California
Bar
Examination

Essay Questions
and
Selected Answers

July 2012

ESSAY QUESTIONS AND SELECTED ANSWERS
JULY 2012
CALIFORNIA BAR EXAMINATION

This publication contains the six essay questions from the July 2012 California Bar Examination and two answers to each question that were written by actual applicants who passed the examination after one read.

The selected answers were assigned good grades and were transcribed for publication as submitted, except that minor corrections in spelling and punctuation were made for ease in reading. The answers are reproduced here with the consent of their authors.

JULY 2012
ESSAY QUESTIONS

California
Bar
Examination

Your answer should demonstrate your ability to analyze the facts in question, to tell the difference between material and immaterial facts, and to discern the points of law and fact upon which the case turns. Your answer should show that you know and understand the pertinent principles and theories of law, their qualifications and limitations, and their relationships to each other.

Your answer should evidence your ability to apply law to the given facts and to reason in a logical, lawyer-like manner from the premises you adopt to a sound conclusion. Do not merely show that you remember legal principles. Instead, try to demonstrate

your proficiency in using and applying them.

If your answer contains only a statement of your conclusions, you will receive little credit. State fully the reasons that support your conclusions, and discuss all points thoroughly.

Your answer should be complete, but you should not volunteer information or discuss legal doctrines which are not pertinent to the solution of the problem.

Unless a question expressly asks you to use California law, you should answer according to legal theories and principles of general application.

Question 1

Pam and Patrick are residents of State A. While visiting State B, they were hit by a truck owned and operated by Corporation, a freight business.

Corporation is incorporated under the laws of Canada and has its headquarters there, where its President and Secretary are located. State B is the only state in which Corporation conducts its business. Corporation's drivers and other employees work out of its warehouse in State B.

Pam and Patrick jointly filed a lawsuit against Corporation in federal district court in State A. In their complaint, Pam demanded damages for personal injury in the amount of $70,000 and for property damage in the amount of $10,000; Patrick demanded damages in the amount of $6,000.

Corporation filed a motion to dismiss the complaint for lack of personal jurisdiction. The federal district court denied the motion. After trial, it entered judgment for Pam in the amount of $60,000 and for Patrick in the amount of $4,000.

Corporation has appealed on the grounds of lack of subject matter jurisdiction and lack of personal jurisdiction.

How should the court of appeals rule on each ground? Discuss.

ANSWER A TO QUESTION 1

1. Did the Federal District Court of State A have Personal Jurisdiction over Corporation?

Waiver?

Personal Jurisdiction is waived if not challenged. Here, Corporation ("Corp") filed a motion to dismiss for lack of personal jurisdiction ("PJ") at trial. Therefore, Corp did not waive its right to appeal based on lack of PJ.

Personal Jurisdiction

Personal jurisdiction is the power of a court to have jurisdiction over an individual or entity. Here, a corporation. The exercise of personal jurisdiction must comport with the requirements of Due Process.

TRADITIONAL BASIS

Traditionally, PJ could only be exercised if the defendant consented to suit in the forum, was served in the forum, or was domiciled in the forum. Here, there are no facts to indicate that Corp consented to jurisdiction ("JDX") because they did not make a general appearance, or in any way consent. Further, Corp is not domiciled in the forum. A corp is domiciled where it has its principal place of business, based on nerve center, and where it is incorporated. Both of those are in Canada for Corp. Finally, facts do not state where Corp was served or if they had an agent for service of process in State A, but assuming that they were not served in state A, there is no traditional basis in state A.

LONG ARM STATUTE

If there is no traditional basis for the exercise of Personal jurisdiction, the court will next look to the state's long-arm statute to determine whether the court has jurisdiction to reach out to another state, or country to exercise jdx over the defendant. Here, there are no facts to indicate that state A has a long-arm. If it did, the federal district court would have jdx to the same extent as the state.

CONSTITUTIONAL ANALYSIS

To comport with due process, personal jurisdiction is only proper if the defendant has such minimum contacts with the forum state that the exercise of jdx comports with traditional notions of fair play and substantial justice.

MINIMUM CONTACTS

Minimum contacts requires a showing of purposeful availment and foreseeability.

PURPOSEFUL AVAILMENT

A party purposefully avails itself of the forum state if it has taken advantage of the benefits and protections of that state's laws. Here, Corporation is incorporated in Canada and has its headquarters there. Further, its warehouse is in state B. Further, Corp oprates a freight business and was driving in state B when the Accident occurred, and state B is the only state in which Corp conducts its business. There are no facts to show that Corporation had any contact at all with state A. Therefore Corp will argue it did not purposefully avail itself of the privileges and benefits of State A.

Foreseeability.

Because State B is the only state in which corp does business, it will argue that it was not foreseeable that it would be haled into court in state A. P and P could argue that a trucking company should foresee being sued anywhere, but if the trucks are only on the road in state B, this argument will not likely prevail. It was not foreseeable that Corp would be sued in state A.

Relatedness of the claim to the contact

The court will look at the quality and nature of the contacts. There is general jurisdiction if the defendant's contact is so systematic and continuous that he is essentially at home in the forum. There is specific jurisdiction if the contact is less than systematic and continuous, but the claim arises out of the defendant's contact with the forum.

Here, there is neither general or specific jdx because the claim neither arises out of the contact with the forum nor is Corp "essentially at home" in the state A because its contact there is not systematic and continuous.

Specifically, the accident occurred while Pam and Patrick were visiting in State B, not state A, and therefore the claim does not arise out of contact with State A, and there can be no Specific Jdx as a result.

Additionally, Corp only does business in State B, has its warehouse in state B and is incorporated and has its president, secretary and headquarters in Canada. Therefore there is no general jdx because there is no contact with State, and certainly not systematic and continuous contact.

Therefore, there is neither specific nor general Jurisdiction.

Fairness

The fairness factors include the convenience of the parties and witnesses as well as the forum state's interest. The court will also look at the interstate judicial system's interest. Although state A has an interest in providing a forum for redress for its citizens, and Pam and Patrick are State A citizens, State B has a stronger interest because that is where the accident occurred, on its roads. Further, because Corp operates in State B only, state B has a strong interest in adjudicating the claims against its citizens for their conduct while in the state. As to convenience, any and all witnesses and evidence would be located in State B, rather than the forum, state A.

Therefore, the fairness factors are in favor of not finding PJ over Corp.

RULING:

Therefore, Under a Due Process Analysis, The court of appeals should rule that there was no personal Jurisdiction over Corp.

2. Did the Federal District Court have Subject Matter Jurisdiction over the matter?
Federal courts are courts of limited jdx and must have jurisdiction under arising under/federal question jurisdiction or diversity jurisdiction.

In some cases, the court may be able to exercise supplemental jurisdiction.

Federal District Court must have had jurisdiction over each and every claim in the matter. Here, both Pam and Patrick brought claims. Therefore, each claim is considered separately below.

WAIVER?

Here, it does not appear that Corporation contested subject matter at trial. However, subject matter is not waived if the party fails to raise it at trial, and may be raised at any time, even on appeal. Therefore, Corporation could appeal based on this ground.

SUBJECT MATTER JURISDICTION OVER PAM'S CLAIM

May have SMJ under either federal question or diversity. Here, the claim arises from personal injury, a tort claim, which is a state claim. Therefore, Pam must show diversity jurisdiction.

Diversity jurisdiction requires complete diversity between the parties (Strawbridge v. Curtiss) and an amount in controversy in excess of $75,000.

COMPLETE DIVERSITY

Complete diversity requires that all plaintiffs are citizens of different states than all defendants. Or, as in the case here, that the suit be between a citizen of a state, and a foreign citizen.

A natural person is a citizen of the state in which she is domiciled. Domicile is physical presence plus intent to remain indefinitely. Here, facts state that Pam is Resident of State A. Therefore, Pam will be domiciled in state A.

A corporation is a dual citizen of every state in which it is incorporated and the state which is its principal place of business. ("PPB") PPB is determined by the "nerve center," or the place from which corporate managers run the corporation. (Hertz v. Friend).

Here, Corp is incorporated under the laws of Canada and thus is a citizen of Canada. Further, Corp has its "nerve center" in Canada because that is where its headquarters is located and where its President and Secretary are located. Although Corp keeps a warehouse in state B and its drivers and other employees work out of the warehouse in state B, no facts indicate that any direction of corporate activity occurs here. Therefore, this is the muscle center, not the nerve center, and the Supreme Court ruled that the Nerve center is the PPB.

Therefore, Corp will be deemed a citizen of Canada, meaning that it is a foreign citizen. Because Pam is a citizen of State A and Corp is a Foreign Citizen of Canada, there is complete diversity between the parties.

AMOUNT IN CONTROVERSY
The amount in controversy must exceed $75,000 exclusive of interests and cost. The plaintiff's good faith claim will control, unless it is clear to a legal certainty that plaintiff cannot recover the required amount (in excess of $75,000).
Here, Pam demanded damages of $70,00 for personal Injury and $10,000 for property damages. Neither amount alone satisfies the amount in controversy.

AGGREGATION
Generally, aggregating claims is not required. However, a single plaintiff may aggregate all claims against a single defendant. This means that Pam can add together

her claims against Corp. Therefore, adding Pam's claims together, her good faith claim was for $80,000. Because there are no facts to indicate this amount was not in good faith, or that there is a legal certainty prohibiting Pam from this recovery (such as a statutory damages cap), Pam has met the amount in controversy.

RESULT IF PLAINTIFF RECOVERS LESS THAN THE AMOUNT IN CONTROVERSY:
If the plaintiff recovers less than the amount in controversy, that will not defeat diversity jdx, because the good faith claim controls. However, in such a case, the plaintiff may be required to pay the defendant's fees in the litigation. Therefore, because Pam recovered on $60,000 that will not defeat diversity, but she may be liable for costs.
RULING:

The federal district court had subject matter jurisdiction over Pam's claim by virtue of diversity jurisdiction. Therefore, the court should deny the appeal based on lack of SMJ over Pam's claim.

SUBJECT MATTER JURISDICTION OVER PATRICK'S CLAIM
As above, this is a tort claim, not arising under federal law, and therefore the court will not have "federal question" jurisdiction. Therefore, Patrick will have to meet the requirements of diversity jurisdiction for the federal district court to have had SMJ.
COMPLETE DIVERSITY

Like Pam above, Patrick is domiciled in state A and will therefore be a citizen of state A. Under the analysis above, Corp is a foreign citizen of Canada. Therefore, as above, there is complete diversity.

AMOUNT IN CONTROVERSY
Patrick requested only $6000 in damages. This is less than $75,000 and therefore does not meet the amount in controversy. Patrick may not aggregate his claim together with Pam, because plaintiffs may not aggregate claims with other plaintiffs.
Therefore, the court did not have diversity jdx over Patrick's claim.

SUPPLEMENTAL JDX

Where the court has jurisdiction over one claim in a matter, it may exercise supplemental jurisdiction over other claims that arise from a Common Nucleus of Operative Fact. The common nucleus test is generally considered broader than the same transaction or occurrence test, and therefore any party that would meet the Same Tran. and Occ. test will meet the Common Nucleus of Operative Fact test.

Here, Pam and Patrick are both suing for injuries and damages arising from the same car accident. While visiting State B, they were hit by a truck owned by Corp, the same truck, in the same accident. The witnesses to both will be the same, as will the evidence. Therefore, Patrick's claim arises from a Common nucleus of operative fact with Pam's claim, and the federal district court could exercise supplemental jdx over Patrick's claim.

DIVERSITY LIMITATIONS ON SUPPLEMENTAL JDX

However, where the underlying claim is in diversity, the court cannot exercise supplemental jdx over a claim by a plaintiff that would defeat complete diversity. Here, Patrick is a plaintiff. However, if supplemental jdx is exercised over Patrick's claim it will not defeat complete diversity because all Plaintiffs will still be citizens of State A, and all Defendants of Canada.

Where the supplemental claim does not meet the amount in controversy, but will not destroy complete diversity, the court may exercise supplemental jurisdiction over the claim. Here, Patrick's claim did not meet the amount in controversy, but will not destroy complete diversity and therefore the court may exercise supplemental jdx over the claim.

DISCRETION

In some cases, a federal district court should exercise discretion not to exercise supplemental jdx, such as where there is a novel or complex issue of state law, or state claims predominate, or all federal questions have been dismissed. On these facts, this is a tort claim for personal injury and therefore not novel or complex. Further, the claim is in diversity and not federal question, and thus there is no concern about the federal claims being dropped out.

This is not a claim over which the court should decline supplemental based on the discretionary factors.

RULING

The Federal district court had subject matter jurisdiction over Patrick's claim based on supplemental jurisdiction. Therefore, the appeals court should deny the motion on the basis of lack of subject matter jurisdiction.

ANSWER B TO QUESTION 1

Pam and Patrick v. Corporation

Pam and Patrick have raised a claim against Corporation (C) in federal district court in State A. Corporation attempted to dismiss the case based on lack of personal jurisdiction (PJ) and subject matter jurisdiction (SMJ). These motions were denied, Pam and Patrick were awarded damages in the case, and Corporation has appealed the case on the grounds listed above. The following considers how the court of appeal should rule on these claims.

Subject Matter Jurisdiction

Subject matter jurisdiction (SMJ) considers whether the court has the power to hear the particular case. This case was brought in federal court; federal courts are courts of limited power, unlike state courts, which can generally hear any case save for several exclusively federal categories. In order for federal courts to have proper SMJ over a case, the case must either be based on a federal question, or meet the requirements for diversity of citizenship jurisdiction. Each of these will be examined in turn to see if the federal courts have jurisdiction over this matter.

Federal Question

A case may properly be held in federal court when the case is based on a federal question. This requires that the plaintiff assert a claim arising under the federal constitution or a federal law. The "well pleaded complaint rule" dictates that the claim be asserted in plaintiff's complaint. It is not enough that a federal issue generally be raised by the case, nor that the defendant will defend on the grounds of a federal law.

Here, the case involves personal injury damages for the injuries that Pam and Patrick suffered when they were hit by a truck owned and operated by Corporation. Thus, it appears that the case is just a simple tort case, which would be based on state law, and not on the constitution or federal law.

Thus, there is no federal question here.

Diversity in Citizenship

However, the federal courts have another means of jurisdiction available, in the form of diversity of citizenship. To be valid, all plaintiffs must be "diverse" in citizenship from all defendants, and the amount in controversy must exceed $75,000.

Diversity

There is an absolute diversity requirement, wherein each plaintiff must be entirely diverse in citizenship from each defendant. The federal rules allow for diversity between citizens of different states, or citizens of a state and a foreign country. Citizenship for individuals is based on their domicile, which is evidenced by physical presence and intent to remain. For corporations, citizenship is determined by place of incorporation, and principal place of business, which is where the owners, directors, and management manage and direct the company's affairs.

Here, Pam and Patrick are residents of State A. Though the facts do not give us any hints into whether they have the intent to remain there, it is reasonable to presume that they did have that intent. Thus, their citizenship is State A.

C is incorporated under the laws of Canada and has its headquarters there, where its President and Secretary are located. Thus, the place of incorporation and the principal place of business is in Canada. Of note, Corporation's drivers and other employees work out of its warehouse in State B. Several years ago, this may have met the "muscle" test, and thus demonstrated citizenship in State B for C; however, this test has been done away with. Nonetheless, there still would be diversity in citizenship even if C was a citizen of State B.

Thus, there is diversity in citizenship, because Pam and Patrick are citizens of State A, and C is a citizen of Canada. Because the rules of civil procedure allow for diversity between residents of a state and a foreign country, there is proper diversity.

Amount in Controversy

Next, the amount in controversy must exceed $75,000 excluding interest and attorney's fees. The court will examine this based off of a good faith pleading of damages by the plaintiff. To reach this amount in controversy, any single plaintiff may aggregate as many claims together to meet the minimum requirement. However, multiple plaintiffs may not aggregate claims in order to reach the minimum requirement.

Here, Pam demanded damages for personal injury in the amount of $70,000, and for property damage in the amount of $10,000. This is an example of aggregation by one plaintiff against one defendant. This is proper. Further, because $70,000 plus $10,000 equals $80,000, it exceeds the amount in controversy requirement.

Patrick demanded damages in the amount of $6,000. This would not be able to be aggregated with Pam's claims in order to reach the amount in controversy; however, because Pam has reached the amount all on the basis of her own claims, this does not impact Patrick's claim. We will need to examine whether Patrick's claim can be joined, however. I will do this later under supplemental jurisdiction (see below).

The conclusion is that the amount in controversy is met, as Pam's claims exceed the required $75,000 minimum amount.

The Effect of Receiving Less Than $75,000 At End Of Trial

C may argue that SMJ was invalid because Pam and Patrick ended up receiving less than $75,000 in damages at the end of the trial. This is incorrect. The mere fact that the parties recovered less than $75,000 at the end of the trial does not mean that the court loses jurisdiction, or never had it in the first place. All that is required is a good faith claim exceeding $75,000. Thus, this will have no effect on the question of SMJ.

Supplemental Jurisdiction: Pat's Claim of $6,000

As discussed above, Pat's claim alone did not meet the amount in controversy requirement. Each and every claim must meet the requirement in order to satisfy SMJ. When the amount in controversy is not met, we can look to supplemental jurisdiction to see if the claim can nonetheless get into federal court.

Supplemental jurisdiction requires that the claim contain a common nucleus of fact with the other claims asserted. If the claim arises out of the same transaction or occurrence, then this test is always met. Supplemental jurisdiction cannot be invoked when it would defeat complete diversity in a diversity case. Here, Pat's claim is based on the exact same incident as Pam - the accident with C's truck. Thus, it is the same transaction or occurrence, and will be able to be heard. The federal courts do have discretion to not hear these claims, but it is likely that they would hear this to get the whole case out of the way at the same time. Further, adding Pat's claim does not defeat diversity, because he is a citizen of State A.

Thus, Pat's claim can properly be heard in federal court.

When Can SMJ Be Asserted?

Finally, we must consider at what point can SMJ be raised as an issue. Some claims must be asserted before certain stages of the trial in order to be preserved, and if not raised, then they are waived. SMJ, however, is never waived, as it is a strict requirement that the federal courts have subject matter jurisdiction. Thus, it is of no concern that C apparently has not raised the SMJ issue prior to the appeal; they can still properly raise it.

Conclusion: The federal court system has proper SMJ over Pam and Patrick's claim.

Personal Jurisdiction

Personal jurisdiction (PJ) considers whether this state can properly hear this claim against this defendant. It asks whether the state has the power to force the defendant to come into the state to defend the claim. To examine whether PJ exists over C in State A, we must look to the traditional bases of exercising jurisdiction, the state long-arm statute, and to the constitutional limitations on exercising PJ.

Traditional Bases of Exercising Jurisdiction

Traditionally, PJ can be asserted over a defendant if the defendant (1) is domiciled in the state; (2) consents to jurisdiction; or (3) is served with process while in the state. As discussed above, C is not domiciled in State A, but is rather domiciled in Canada. Further, it does not appear that C has consented to jurisdiction in State A in any way (though we will later talk about the need to timely raise the argument of lack of personal jurisdiction). And finally, there is no indication that C was served in State A.

Thus, the traditional bases of exercising jurisdiction seem to not be present.

Long-Arm Statute

A long-arm statute is a state statute that states when the state can reach and "grab" an out-of-state defendant, and force the defendant to defend in the state court. Some of these long-arm statutes require that the defendant commit a tortuous act in the state, or break a contract in the state, while others simply grant the state the ability to reach out to grab defendants to the full extent as allowed by the U.S. Constitution.

Here, the facts do not mention the reach of State A's long-arm statute. It is reasonable to assume that it reaches the constitutional limits. Thus, we must examine the constitutional limits of PJ.

Constitutional Limitations

To exert PJ over an out-of-state defendant, the constitution requires certain minimum contacts with the forum state such that maintenance of the suit there does not offend traditional notions of fair play and substantial justice. To determine if this is true in this case, we can break the above test down Into three sections: minimum contacts, relatedness of the claim to the contact, and fairness.

Minimum Contacts

The constitutional requires the defendant to have some minimum contacts with the forum state in order for the state to exert jurisdiction. The defendant must have purposefully availed himself in the state, such that being subject to a claim in that state would be foreseeable.

Purposeful Availment

Purposeful availment requires that the defendant commit a voluntary act in the forum state. Defendant must avail himself in some way to the state, whether it be by using the state's roads, or attempting to make money in the state.

Here, C is incorporated in Canada, and has its principal place of business there. It conducts business solely in State B, which is also where it has a warehouse. Further, the accident occurred in State B. It is possible that C drives on State A roads from time to time, but the facts do not give this information. Also, there are no facts which say that C ships goods to State A, or otherwise tries to make money there. Simply put, on these facts, there seem to be no contacts whatsoever with State A, other than that Pam and Patrick are residents of State A.

The court of appeal should find that there was no purposeful availment.

Foreseeability

The minimum contacts must be sufficient enough to make it foreseeable that defendant would be "haled into court" in the forum state. Here, as discussed, there appears to be nothing that C did that would make it foreseeable that they would end up in State A. The mere fact of driving on State B's roads does not make it foreseeable that they would end up in State A's court. I suppose if State A were located directly adjacent to State B that it would perhaps be more foreseeable, but again, the facts do not share that information. A case against C in State A court was not foreseeable.

Relatedness of the Claim to the Contact

The more related the claim is to the contact with the forum state, the more likely the court will be to allow for jurisdiction over the defendant.

If the claim arises directly out of the contact with the forum state, this gives rise to specific personal jurisdiction. Here, there was no contact with State A, and so there cannot be specific jurisdiction.

Next, general personal jurisdiction may exist if the defendant consistently and regularly conducts activity in the forum state, such that he is "essentially at home there." Merely selling goods in a state does not give rise to general PJ, there must be an actual physical presence. Here, C is not in State A whatsoever, or so it seems. Thus, it is not essentially at home in State A. It may essentially be at home in State B, where it has a warehouse, but this does not affect the discussion of whether State A has jurisdiction. The claim is not related to C's contact with State A, as C has no contact with State A.

Fairness

Finally, the court will look to see if holding the suit in the state meets general standards of fairness. Under this, the court considers convenience to the parties and the witnesses, the forum state's interests, and the plaintiff's interests.

Convenience

Under the convenience factor, the court will look to see how convenient it is to hold the case in the forum state, based on a variety of factors including where the parties are, where the witnesses are, where the evidence is, etc. If the inconvenience to the defendant grossly impacts his ability to defend against the case, the court will likely dismiss for lack of PJ.

Here, the accident occurred in State B, so any witnesses are likely in State B. It is unknown where the wreckage is located, but the vehicles are likely also in State B. Thus, a good portion of the pertinent materials needed would be in State B. Further, C has no connection with State A, and will have to travel there to defend against the suit. This is likely not entirely burdensome, because they are a corporation, and likely would have the resources to get there.

However, it was likely entirely inconvenient to have the case in State A, based on where the evidence, witnesses, and the defendant was located.

State's Interests

Next, the court will look to see if the forum state has a strong interest in providing a forum for the claim. Here, State A is interested in providing a forum for its residents; it wants to be sure that they are compensated for their injuries. However, the accident occurred on State B's roads, and so State B would have more of an interest, because it wants to be sure that dangerous drivers are kept off of their roads.

In the end, a court would likely find that State A has a limited interest in holding this case.

Plaintiff's Interests

Finally, the court looks to the plaintiff's interests in having the case in the forum state. It is likely that Pam and Patrick have suffered some injuries and thus would prefer to not have to travel. However, they had already been in State B on vacation, and could likely travel there again if needed. The court generally will be deferential to the plaintiff's choice of forum, however.

In the end, it is likely that it is simply not fair to have C defend in State A court.

When Can PJ Be Asserted?

On a final note, PJ must be asserted either in a 12b motion prior to the answer, or along with the answer. If not, it is waived. Here, it appears that C raised the PJ motion at some point early on, and thus likely did not waive it, so that it can be heard on appeal. Some courts require that a party immediately appeal a decision on PJ by way of an extraordinary writ.

Conclusion:

The Court of Appeal should hold the court had SMJ over the matter, but not PJ. Thus, provided that PJ has not been waived, it should dismiss the case. If it has been waived, the court should reject the PJ argument as well.

Question 2

Wendy and Hal are married and live in California.

A year ago, Wendy told Hal that she would not tolerate his drinking any longer. She insisted that he move out of the family home and not return until he completed an alcohol treatment program. He moved out but did not obtain treatment.

Last month, Hal went on a drinking spree, started driving, and struck a pedestrian. When Wendy learned of the accident, she told Hal that she wanted a divorce.

Hal has consulted Lawyer about defending him in a civil action filed by the pedestrian. He is currently unemployed. His only asset is his interest in the family home, which he and Wendy purchased during their marriage. Lawyer offered to represent Hal if Hal were to give him a promissory note, secured by a lien on the family home, for his fees. Hal immediately accepted.

1. Is Wendy's interest in the family home subject to damages recovered for injuries to the pedestrian? Discuss. Answer according to California law.

2. Is Wendy's interest in the family home subject to payment of Hal's legal fees? Discuss. Answer according to California Law.

3. What, if any, ethical violations has Lawyer committed? Discuss. Answer according to California and ABA authorities.

ANSWER A TO QUESTION 2

1. Is Wendy's Interest in the Family Home Subject to Damages Recovered for Injuries to the Pedestrian?

California is a Community Property State

California is a community property (CP) jurisdiction. Thus, any property acquired by either spouse during the course of the marriage by either spouse's labor is presumptively community property. Property acquired before or after the marriage by either spouse, or during the marriage by gift, inheritance, or devise, is presumptively separate property (SP). In determining the character of a particular asset, it is helpful to look at (1) the source of the asset or the source of the funds used to purchase the asset, (2) any actions by the spouses changing the character of the property, and (3) any relevant presumptions.

The House

Source

The facts tell us that Wendy (W) and Hal (H) purchased the family house during their marriage. However, we don't know what funds were used to purchase the house. If W's or H's earnings were used (or a combination thereof), and those earnings were earned during the course of the marriage, then the house would be CP because spousal earnings are CP to the extent they're earned during the marriage.

However, if one spouse partially used inheritance money or other SP acquired before the marriage, then that spouse would likely have a SP interest in the home to the extent SP was used to purchase it.

However, without more, the best assumption is that spousal earnings were used to purchase the house. The facts say H is currently unemployed, but he may have been employed in the past (and thus had earnings). Further, we can assume W earned money somehow, likely from a job.

23

Actions

There is no evidence that the house was put in only one spouse's name, suggesting that the house was the separate property of that spouse. Pre-1975, if the house was in W's name, the married woman's special presumption would operate to render the house (or the share of the house in W's name) W's SP.

Modernly, if title was taken in only one spouse's name, a court would not likely hold that to be conclusive evidence that the house was that spouse's SP absent some manifestation by the other spouse that the house was intended as a gift.

If H and W took title to the house as joint tenants with a right of survivorship, each would have a 1/2 SP undivided interest in the whole during life. On death, the form of title would control. On divorce, under CA's anti-Lucas statute, the house would be treated as CP, with a right to reimbursement for any SP used by either spouse to improve the home.

Finally, there's no evidence of a transmutation changing the character of the house, which, after 1985, would have to be in writing.

Thus, absent any of these actions, it appears the house is still CP.

Presumption

All property acquired during the course of marriage is presumptively CP. Here, nothing rebuts that presumption.

Community Responsibility for Debts of One Spouse

All debts incurred by either spouse prior to or during the course of marriage are community debts. Tort obligations are "incurred" when the tort occurs, not when judgment is handed down. Thus, any obligations arising out of H striking the pedestrian were "incurred" when he hit the pedestrian.

W will argue that the marital economic community was not in existence when H hit the pedestrian because she had kicked him out of the house. The marital economic community begins at marriage and terminates upon permanent physical separation when at least one spouse has no intent of continuing the marriage.

Here, W kicked H out of the house. However, she told him that he could return when he completed an alcohol abuse program. Thus, the marital economic community had not yet ended when H got in the accident because W was still open to the possibility of him returning. W will argue that H manifested an intent to never continue the marriage because he refused to go to treatment. In other words, W will argue that by rejecting the pre-condition to the continuation of the marriage--i.e. getting treatment--H effectively terminated the marital economic community. Indeed, W can point to the fact that 11 months after she kicked H out, he hadn't obtained treatment. Given this length of time, W can argue, it's clear that the community had ended.

However, the stronger argument is that the marital economic community continued until W told H that she wanted a divorce. If W viewed the marital community as over prior to the accident, she would have likely filed for divorce then. Instead, it appears the accident was the "last straw." Thus, the request for a divorce was the clearest signal by either party that the physical separation was permanent and there was no intent to continue the marriage.

Thus, the marital economic community had not ended when H struck the pedestrian, any obligation incurred because of the accident is a community debt.

Order of Payment

When a tort is committed during an activity for the benefit of the community, the debt will be satisfied first by CP, then by the tortfeasor's SP. The non-tortfeasor spouse's SP is not subject to the debt.

When a tort is not committed during an activity for the benefit of the community, the debt will be satisfied first by the tortfeasor's SP, then by CP. Again, the other spouse's SP is safe.

Here, H committed the tort against the pedestrian while driving drunk. This was not an activity for the benefit of the community--to the contrary, H was supposed to be seeking alcohol abuse treatment while he was living away from the family home. Thus, recovery would be taken out of H's SP before the CP.

However, on the facts, it doesn't seem as though H has any SP to satisfy the debt. Thus, any recovery will likely be against the H and W's CP.

Reimbursement to the Community

To the extent any CP--i.e. the house--is used to pay any obligation arising out of H's accident with the pedestrian, the community may be entitled to reimbursement from H. Where CP is used to pay an obligation arising out of spouse's tort that was committed not during an activity for the benefit of the community, the community is entitled to reimbursement for that payment if the tortfeasor's SP was available to pay (or if the order of payment was not followed). However, as mentioned, it doesn't appear H has any SP available to pay the debt and, thus, reimbursement may be unlikely.

Distribution of Debts on Divorce

At divorce, community assets are generally divided under the "equal division rule"--i.e. each spouse gets 1/2 of each community asset in kind.

However, a judge has more discretion as to the allocation of debts at divorce. Typically, a judge will allocate a tort debt to the tortfeasor spouse if the tort was incurred not during an activity for the benefit of the community. However, a judge may take into account ability to pay to effect a more just allocation of debts.

Here, on divorce, the judge would likely allocate any judgment based on H striking the pedestrian to H. H will argue that he's unemployed and can't pay, but it's highly unlikely a judge would saddle W with an obligation to pay H's tort liability post-divorce.

Conclusion

Thus, during the marriage, H and W's CP will be liable for damages recovered for injuries to the pedestrian. Even though H and W have filed for divorce, until community assets and debts are distributed, the community estate continues and the pedestrian can recover against it. However, as mentioned, on divorce, the debt will be allocated to H. Further, W may be entitled to reimbursement for CP used to pay the debt.

*Note: If the court decided that the marital community was terminated when H struck the pedestrian, then CP--i.e. the house--would not be liable for the debt because the debt would be H's SP.

2. Is Wendy's Interest in the Family Home Subject to Payment of H's Legal Fees

Equal Management

Each spouse generally has equal rights to manage community property. This includes the right to sell and encumber community property. However, with respect to real property, one spouse may not encumber community owned real property without the other spouse's consent. If one spouse, without consent, sells or encumbers community real estate, the non-consenting spouse has the power to void that transaction within 1 year.

Lien on the House

Here, H has given Lawyer a lien on the family home without W's consent. Thus, W has the power within 1 year to void the encumbrance.

H will argue that because he gave the lien on the house after W told him she wanted a divorce, he was only granting a lien on his 1/2 SP interest in the family home. However, there's no evidence that W actually filed for divorce or that divorce proceedings were held during which a judge divided the community estate. While the marital economic community may no longer exist because there has been permanent physical separation, the community estate lives on until it has been distributed.

Thus, a court would likely allow W to void the encumbrance on the community real property due to her lack of consent in making the encumbrance.

Timing of the Attorney's Fees

Furthermore, H sought legal advice after W told him she wanted a divorce. Because W asking for divorce terminated the marital economic community, CP--i.e. the family home--is not liable for the debts incurred by H after such separation.

Thus, any obligation owed to Lawyer based on legal services rendered to H cannot be satisfied out of CP because such an obligation would not be a community debt.

He would argue that payment of attorney's fees is an obligation arising out of the accident of the pedestrian, when the marital economic community still existed. However, the attorney's fees represent an entirely different event. Furthermore, contractual obligations arise when the contract was made. Here, any contract and/or agreement with Lawyer was made after the economic community ended. Therefore, W's interest in the family home is not subject to payment for the additional reason that CP is not liable for H's separate post-marriage debts.

Necessaries

Post-separation, a spouse can still be liable for obligations relating to necessaries that the other spouse incurred during the marriage. Necessaries generally refer to food, shelter, and medical expenses. Here, H's legal fees don't likely constitute necessaries and, as such, this theory cannot be invoked to hold W's interest in the family home subject to payment.

3. Lawyer's Ethical Violations

Obtaining Pecuniary Interest in Outcome of Case

Under the ABA, a lawyer cannot obtain a pecuniary interest in the subject matter of a case other than in the case of a contingency fee arrangement or an attorney's lien. However, in CA, attorneys' liens are impermissible.

Here, Lawyer effectively acquired an attorney's lien on H's family home. Thus, Lawyer will argue that this was permissible because the only purpose here was to secure payment. In CA, this would constitute an ethical violation. Under the ABA, it's less clear.

While under the ABA, an attorney's lien is permissible, if Lawyer knew that H couldn't rightfully encumber the family home, then it's possible that Lawyer committed an ethical violation because accepting the attorney's lien would constitute a violation of a third party's (W's) rights in the course of representing H.

Entering into Business Transactions with Clients

An attorney can only enter a business transaction with a client if (1) the terms are fair and reasonable, (2) the terms are communicated to the client in an easily understandable manner, (3) the client is advised to get independent counsel to represent him in the transaction and is given a chance to do so, and (4) the client consents.

Here, by taking a lien on H's family home, Lawyer entered into a business transaction with H. However, it's not clear that Lawyer ever advised H to seek independent counsel or that he adequately informed him of the material terms of the lien. Although H immediately accepted, he did so without knowing what would trigger enforcement of the lien (1 missed payment? total failure to pay? late payment? H's insolvency?). Thus, by failing to adequately inform H and encouraging him to seek independent advice, Lawyer likely violated the ethics rules.

Fees

Under the ABA, a fee must be reasonable. In CA, fees can't be unconscionable. Further, in CA, a fee agreement must be in writing unless it's (1) less than $1k, (2) with a corporation, or (3) for a routine matter involving an existing client.

Here, the lien agreement was essentially a fee agreement. However, the terms were not adequately disclosed to H. Further, there was no written fee agreement. Because a writing was likely required--there's no evidence H was an existing client or that Lawyer's services were valued at under $1k--this is a violation of CA rules.

Further, the lien was likely unreasonable and unconscionable. Because H was unemployed, it was extremely unlikely that he was going to be able to pay Lawyer's fees. If Lawyer knew that H was unemployed--which he likely did, considering he conditioned representing H on having a lien on the house--then Lawyer must have known that H wouldn't be able to pay. Thus, the fee agreement was unconscionable because it was akin to a mortgagee lending to a mortgagor knowing that the mortgagor was going to default and the foreclosure was inevitable. Lawyer must have known (a) that H wasn't going to be able to pay and (b) that the value of the lien on the home was worth more than the value of the services to be provided.

Thus, the fee arrangement likely constituted an ethical violation.

Violating Rights of Third Parties

Lawyers cannot violate the rights of third parties in the course of representing a client. To the extent the lien violates W's rights and Lawyer knew of this, he likely acted unethically. Furthermore, if Lawyer knew that H could not rightfully encumber the family house, then Lawyer arguably breached his duty of competent and candid representation by not informing H that he couldn't offer a lien on his house without W's consent.

ANSWER B TO QUESTION 2

1. **Is Wendy's interest in the family home subject to damages recovered for injuries to the pedestrian hit by Hal under California law?**

The parties were married and live in California. Thus, their property rights as a couple, specifically with regard to the property acquired during the marriage, are governed by California community property law. Whether the house was community or separate property can be determined by the source of the asset, whether any presumptions apply, and the actions of the parties during the marriage.

Community Presumption

There is a community presumption regarding property acquired during the marriage that it is community property. This would apply to the family home given, as the facts state, it was acquired during the marriage. The presumption can be rebutted by a showing that the house was not actually acquired during the marriage, it was acquired during the marriage but with separate property funds, the house was a gift/devise/inheritance, or the house was the rent/issue/profit derived from separate property.

Their house was purchased during the marriage so it was not a gift or devise. Although it is possible that the house was purchased with separate property funds, there are no facts to indicate this was the case. Because it was purchased during the marriage, and there are no facts to rebut the presumption, the house is considered community property.

Judgments Against Spouses

A tort judgment against a spouse will subject both the community property and the separate property of the tortfeasor to the judgment. But once the community property is divided, debt cannot be recovered from the spouse who received her half of the community property from what she received under the divorce decree unless she was the spouse that incurred the debt or the debt was assigned to her. Thus, for a judgment against Hal for drinking and driving, the community will be liable for this debt, and it can be satisfied from the community property.

For the Benefit of the Community

Although the community property is liable for the judgment by the pedestrian, the judgment must be satisfied first from the separate property of the tortfeasor spouse if the tort was not committed by conduct that was being performed for the benefit of the community. For example, if Hal was on his way to drop the kids off at school or to pay the mortgage on the house, this would be for the benefit of the community. In that case, the judgment would be satisfied first from community property, and if there was any deficiency, then from the separate property of the tortfeasor.

Here, Hal had been kicked out [of] the house for his drinking problem at the time of the accident. Wendy had clearly communicated her disapproval for Hal's drinking. The drinking, including drinking and driving, would actually harm, not benefit, the community. Although we do not know where Hal was headed, he had already been kicked out of the house and was, generally, involved in a drinking binge at the time. Therefore, his actions were not to the benefit of the community and can be satisfied first from his separate property assets.

But the facts state that his only asset, at the present time, is his interest in the family home. Because it appears he has no separate property from which to satisfy the judgment, the judgment will be satisfied from the community property home.

End of the Economic Community

The accident in which the pedestrian was hit occurred after Hal had been kicked out of the house but before Wendy told Hal she wanted a divorce. As stated above, the source of property or debt, whether it was incurred before, during or after the marriage, can indicate whether it is community or separate debt. The pedestrian's claim is a form of debt because, once rendered, the plaintiff can reduce it to a judgment and attach liens to the tortfeasor's property. Thus, the question arises whether the economic community ended when Wendy kicked Hal out of the house, because if so, the injury and judgment would have occurred after the economic community ended and would be the separate debt of Hal. In this case, the judgment could not be satisfied from community property, including the house.

In California, end of the economic community occurs when there is physical separation and an intent not to carry on the marital relationship anymore. If the parties maintain the facade or marriage, although physically separated, the economic community will not be considered to be at an end. The economic community will certainly result, if the above elements are not satisfied, when the divorce decree is entered.

Here, Wendy kicked Hal out of the house one year ago. She did not say anything about ending the marriage or never wanting to see him again. She did tell him he could not return until he completed alcohol treatment. Thus, Hal being kicked out was not indicative of an intent to permanently end the marriage relationship, it was indicative of a temporary physical separation by Wendy for the limited purpose of motivating Hal to get treatment and save the marriage. Thus the economic community would not have ended simply when he left the house.

But, after having moved out and hitting the pedestrian while drinking, Wendy learned of the accident and told Hal she wanted a divorce. At this point, both elements would be met. Hal and Wendy would have been physically separated, and one spouse has indicated an intention not to resume the marital relation by telling the other she wants a divorce.

Because the economic community did not end until that time, when Wendy told Hal she wanted a divorce, and the accident and/or the cause of action that is the basis for any judgment accrued before that time, the judgment resulting would be a community debt because it was essentially incurred before the end of the economic community.

33

Debt

Debt incurred before or during the marriage can be satisfied from the community or from the tortfeasor's separate property. Debt incurred by a spouse for necessaries, including medical care, can be satisfied from community property or the separate property of either spouse, although indemnity may be available. Here, the debt is for tort judgment and, as stated above, can be satisfied from either community property or separate property of Hal, first from his separate property and then from the community property. In California, for the purpose of debt for necessaries or medical services, end of the economic community can only occur on divorce. Judgment may not be able to be satisfied from Wendy's earnings if she kept them in a separate (versus joint) account from which Hal had no right of withdrawal.

CONCLUSION--Because the debt was incurred before end of the economic community, it is a community debt. Therefore, it can be satisfied from community property or separate property of Hal. Because the tort that is the basis of the judgment was not conducted for the benefit of the community, the judgment must be satisfied first from Hal's separate property. But because Hal has no separate property, his only asset is the house, it will be reduced to judgment and recovery sought from the asset that is the community home, which as above is classified as community property. Wendy may be able to seek indemnity.

2. Is Wendy's interest in the family home subject to payment of Hal's legal fees under California law?

As stated above, the economic community ended when Wendy kicked Hal out of the house and told him she wanted a divorce. Hal appears from the facts to have consulted the lawyer after that time. Debt incurred after the end of the economic community will belong to the debtor spouse.

Attorney Fees for Divorce Lawyer

Generally, a spouse may not unilaterally encumber community real property without a joint action on behalf of both spouses. Additionally, the spouse may not separately encumber her half interest in the property. The one exception to this rule is for the spouse to satisfy attorney fees in the divorce proceeding between the spouses.

Here, because the lawyer is not representing Hal as a family attorney in his anticipated divorce proceeding with Wendy, this rule would not apply. The lawyer fees incurred by Hal after the economic community ended for the purpose of defending against the tort suit could only be satisfied from Hal's separate property.

Division of Assets on Divorce

Generally, assets are divided pro rata at divorce, 50-50, no cashing out one spouse to give the other an entire asset. The only general exceptions to this rule are: for a closely held corporation whose shares are community assets where one spouse is the CEO and division would destroy the business; a pension plan from which one spouse can take a cashout instead of receiving payments from the pension so the spouse, who no longer wish to have any connection can go their separate ways; or, for the family home when selling it and dividing the proceeds will uproot the children and cause them harm.

While this is the family home, there appear to be no children and no reason not to apply the binding pro rata division, 50-50, by sale of the house and splitting the assets.

This means that on divorce, the assets of the house will be split evenly between the parties. Once the divorce decree is entered, the proceeds from the house that Hal receives are going to be his separate property. Upon divorce, the legal fees of Hal's lawyer can be paid by his share of the proceeds.

But the question asks whether the payment of Hal's legal fees will be satisfied from Wendy's interest in the home. Wendy has no interest in Hal's proceeds after divorce from sale of the community property house, and thus the proceeds subject Hal's interest, not hers, to liability.

CONCLUSION--because the attorney fee debt will have been incurred after end of the economic community, it will be separate debt of Hal, and does not subject any of Wendy's interest in the family home to liability for those fees. The exception for divorce attorney fees does not apply.

3. **What ethical violations has the lawyer committed according to both the ABA and California law?**

A lawyer is a fiduciary of the client. She has a duty of confidentiality (not to communicate information relating to representation), a duty of loyalty not to act on behalf of her own, a client's, or a third party's best interests that are adverse to her client's, financial duties, and duties of competence which are all owed to the client.

Duty of Loyalty

Under the duty of loyalty, the lawyer must not develop an interest or maintain an interest that is adverse to the client, whether it is the interest of the lawyer herself, an interest of one of the lawyer's other clients, or an interest of a third party with whom the lawyer is closely related.

Loyalty--Financial Assistance to Clients

Under the ABA rules, a lawyer is not permitted to lend the client money for the representation, with the exception of forwarding costs of litigation to indigent clients and forwarding costs associated with a contingent fee arrangement. Under the California rules, the lawyer can lend the client any amount for any reason, as long as she does not promise to satisfy the existing debts of the client in order to buy the client's business.

Therefore, from this perspective, the loan would be considered acceptable under the California rules but unacceptable under the ABA rules. Under the ABA rules, once the client becomes indebted to the attorney, the attorney's personal interest against the client in collecting the money and receiving payment for the debt may conflict with his duty to act for the sole benefit of the client. Under the California rules, because this is not a promise to satisfy pre-existing debt for the prospective client, this is acceptable.

Loyalty--Transacting Business or Developing Adverse Interest to Client

Whenever the lawyer enters into business with the client, the terms must be fair, the lawyer must disclose the terms (effect of the transaction) to the client in writing, allow for an opportunity for the client to consult with independent counsel and probably should suggest she do so if the lawyer's interest will be adverse to the client's in the litigation, and obtain consent from the client in writing.

This loan would essentially be such a transaction. The facts do not indicate the above elements are met. Additionally, there is a question whether it would be fair to encumber a client's sole asset in order to receive payment. But the above rules that specifically address lending a client money are going to govern whether the transaction is permissible. Regardless, even though the loan is permissible under California law, the attorney should ethically consider whether the terms of the loan are fair and suggest receiving independent legal advice if the client wishes to fund the representation in this manner.

Financial Duties

The reason the nature of the fee arrangement is important is to judge whether it is permissible for the lawyer to charge the client in this way. Under the ABA, the fee must be reasonable considering the experience of the lawyer, novelty of the case, difficulty of legal issues, time and effort required, etc. In California, it simply must not be unconscionable. The question is whether the lawyer has complied with the requirements for charging a fee, and whether the amount is justified.

Contingent Fee

A lawyer can enter into either an hourly fee arrangement or a contingent fee arrangement with a client, or potentially a flat fee arrangement. Under the ABA rules, contingent fee arrangements (lawyer forwards fees and sometimes costs in order for a stake in the recovery, if there happens to be one) are not available in criminal or domestic cases. They must include the percentage of recovery taken, the costs deducted from recovery, and whether they are deducted before or after. In California, the agreement must also indicate that it is subject to negotiation with the lawyer and what costs will not be covered by the contingent fee arrangement.

Under ABA rules, this may be a criminal case, but considering the question implies a money judgment that could subject the house to liability, brought by a private party pedestrian; using contingent fee arrangement in this case would be permissible. But here, if the mortgage is being used as payment, and thus this is more likely to be considered an hourly fee arrangement.

Hourly Fee

The agreement, under ABA rules, must disclose the rate at which the fee is charged, the services it covers, and the respective duties of lawyer and client. In California, it must also be in writing unless it is for less than $1,000, with a corporate client, routine matter for regular client, or emergency renders this impossible.

CONCLUSION--There is nothing in the facts to indicate the lawyer has complied with any of the above requirements regarding the fee arrangement. He made the offer to encumber the property without explaining the calculation of the rate, providing a writing, explaining what services it would cover, etc. Additionally, the case appears to be a simple one, involving culpability for drunk driving. Depending on how much the house was worth, a lien on the home could be unreasonable or unconscionable under either California or ABA approach.

Duty of Competence

A lawyer has a duty of competence, to represent the client with the skill, knowledge, thoroughness and preparation necessary to carry out the representation effectively.

As stated above, the home is community property. It cannot be encumbered unless both spouses jointly enter into the transaction. The non-consenting spouse can recover the house even from a BFP, and set aside the transaction, if she has not agreed to it.

There is a one year statute of limitations, but if the buyer knew the seller was married and failed to seek consent from the other spouse, there is no statute of limitations.

Here, an attempt to encumber the community property house to satisfy the separate debt of Hal would be a failure of competence on the part of the lawyer. A lawyer of reasonable skill, knowledge, thoroughness and preparation would be aware of this and would not attempt to encumber property to pay his debts knowing it was community property not subject to this type of transaction without consent of Wendy. This would ineffectively carry out the representation.

CONCLUSION--Under ABA rules only, the lawyer has breached his duty of loyalty to the client by lending him money in regard to the transaction. Although, he may argue he is permitted to do so because he is permitted to forward costs of litigation to indigent clients and Hal is indigent because he is unemployed and has no assets but the house. But because the house cannot be encumbered this way without the consent of Wendy, and a lawyer of reasonable skill and knowledge would know this, the attempt to encumber the house without Wendy's permission may also be a breach of duty of competence, subjecting the lawyer to discipline, sanctions, and malpractice liability. There is also a question of whether the amount of the fee is reasonable or unconscionable in light of the nature of the litigation and employment of the lawyer.

Question 3

Vicky was killed on a rainy night. The prosecution charged Dean, a business rival, with her murder. It alleged that, on the night in question, he hid in the bushes outside her home and shot her when she returned from work.

At Dean's trial in a California court, the prosecution called Whitney, Dean's wife, to testify. One week after the murder, Whitney had found out that Dean had been dating another woman and had moved out, stating the marriage was over. Still angry, Whitney was willing to testify against Dean. After Whitney was called to the stand, the court took a recess. During the recess, Dean and Whitney reconciled. Whitney decided not to testify against Dean. The trial recommenced and the prosecutor asked Whitney if she saw anything on Dean's shoes the night of the murder. When Whitney refused to answer, the court threatened to hold her in contempt. Reluctantly, Whitney testified that she saw mud on Dean's shoes.

The prosecution then called Ella, Dean's next-door neighbor. Ella testified that, on the night Vicky was killed, she was standing by an open window in her kitchen, which was about 20 feet from an open window in Dean's kitchen. She also testified that she saw Dean and Whitney and she heard Dean tell Whitney, "I just killed the gal who stole my biggest account." Dean and Whitney did not know that Ella overheard their conversation.

Dean called Fred, a friend, to testify. Fred testified that, on the day after Vicky was killed, he was having lunch in a coffee shop when he saw Hit, a well-known gangster, conversing at the next table with another gangster, Gus. Fred testified that he heard Gus ask Hit if he had "taken care of the assignment concerning Vicky," and that Hit then drew his index finger across his own throat.

Assuming all appropriate objections and motions were timely made, did the court properly:

   1. Allow the prosecution to call Whitney? Discuss.

   2. Admit the testimony of:
      (a) Whitney? Discuss.
      (b) Ella? Discuss.
      (c) Fred? Discuss.

Answer according to California law.

Answer A to Question 3

California Proposition 8: Truth in Evidence Rule

Under Proposition 8 in California, all non-privileged, relevant evidence is admissible in a criminal prosecution brought in California unless it falls within one of the specified exceptions to the rule. Evidence that is admissible under Proposition 8 is still subject to CEC 352 balancing.

Here, as this case involves the prosecution charging Dean with murder, Proposition 8 will apply to admit any evidence that is relevant and is not excluded for CEC 352 balancing.

1. Allow the Prosecution to call Whitney

The first issue is whether the prosecution should be allowed to call Whitney. This depends on whether Whitney ("W") can claim one of the spousal privileges: spousal communications privilege or spousal testimonial privilege.

Spousal Communications Privilege

The spousal communications privilege protects all confidential communications between spouses that are made in the course of an existing marriage and in reliance on the intimacy of the marriage. This privilege belongs to both spouses and may be claimed by either to prevent the other spouse from testifying. Moreover, the privilege exists regardless of whether the marriage has ended in divorce, so long as the communication itself was made during a period when the marriage existed. For purposes of the privilege, marriage does not end until there is a valid divorce.

Here, Whitney was called by the prosecution to testify that she saw mud on Dean's shoes. This observation occurred when Dean and W were still married as Dean and W have yet to obtain a divorce and reconciled prior to W providing any testimony. Although W and D had separated because W had discovered that D was dating another woman and W had moved out, for the purpose of this privilege, it extends for any

41

communication made prior to divorce. Finally, as W was called to testify to an observation, rather than a communication between W and Dean, it would not be protected under the communications privilege.

Thus, this privilege would not apply to prevent W from testifying as she did or to prevent her from taking the stand.

Spousal Testimonial Privilege

The spousal testimonial privilege allows one spouse to refuse to testify against another spouse in any action. For this privilege to apply, a valid marriage must still exist. The privilege belongs to the testifying spouse, as the privilege is designed to protect the harmony of the marriage, which is not salvageable if the testifying spouse wishes to testify. Moreover, in California, the privilege allows the testifying spouse to avoid taking the stand entirely.

Here, W was called to the stand to testify that she saw mud on D's shoes during the night of the murder. Although W and D had been separated, because W moved out and stated the marriage was over when she discovered that D had been dating another woman and moved out, the marriage had not ended for the purposes of the privilege, which requires a valid divorce. As such, W was privileged to choose not to take the stand.

In this case, W initially was angry and was willing to testify against D and thus agreed to take the stand and testify. W actually took the stand and was sworn in, prior to the recess in which W and D reconciled and W decided not to offer testimony. Thus, the prosecution will argue that W waived the privilege because she took the stand and was sworn under oath.

By contrast, W will assert that she did not waive the privilege because, although she took the stand, she asserted the privilege the first time that she was asked a question by the prosecution. W refused to answer when court resumed and the prosecutor asked W if she saw anything on D's shoes at the night of the murder.

As W asserted the privilege prior to answering any questions, the court will find that she had a spousal testimonial privilege and could not be forced to testify against D. However, W took the stand voluntarily and thus it was proper to allow the prosecution to call W because she was the holder of the privilege and had not yet claimed it. Proposition 8 does not allow privileged information to be admitted and thus will not change the outcome.

2. Admit the Testimony

(a) Whitney

The first issue is whether the court should have admitted the testimony of Whitney.

Logical Relevance

Under California law, evidence is relevant if it makes a fact of consequence that is actually in dispute more or less probable then it would be without the evidence.

Here, W testified that she saw mud on D's shoes. As V was killed on a rainy night, and the prosecution was arguing that D hid in the bushes outside her home and shot her when she returned from work, this evidence would make it more likely that D was present in a muddy flowerbed and committed the murder.

Thus, it is relevant.

Legal Relevance

Evidence is legally relevant if its probative value is not substantially outweighed by the danger of unfair prejudice, confusion of the issues, misleading the jury, waste, or undue delay.

Here, D will argue that the testimony about mud on his shoes is likely to confuse and mislead the jury, particularly if the prosecution has failed to establish that the mud came from a flowerbed near Vicky's home. However, as this evidence has high probative value in that it shows that D was standing outside in mud on a rainy night, it will likely be admitted. Thus, this objection will fail.

Personal Knowledge

In order to be competent to testify, a witness must have personal knowledge of the facts to which she is testifying based upon her percipient observations.

Here, W saw mud on D's shoes in the night in question and thus testimony about the state of the shoes is within her perception and personal knowledge.

Spousal Communications Privilege

As discussed above, this will not protect W's testimony about the mud on D's shoes as it was not a communication, but was an observation.

Spousal Testimonial Privilege

As discussed above, this will protect W's testimony because she is still married to D and therefore cannot be compelled to offer evidence against him in the criminal action. Prop 8 does not change the outcome as privileged information is excluded.

Conclusion

W's testimony will be excluded as a result of the spousal testimonial privilege.

(b) Ella

The second issue is the admissibility of Ella's testimony.

Logical Relevance

See rule above.

Ella's testimony that she overheard D tell W that he "just killed the gal who stole my biggest account" is highly relevant to the case. D is charged with murder and his alleged motivation for killing Vicky is that they were business rivals. The statement thus indicates that D committed V's murder, particularly because it was made on the night that V was killed. This fact is in dispute as it relates to whether or not D is guilty of the crime with which he is charged. Thus, this testimony is logically relevant.

Legal Relevance
See rule above.

Although D will argue that this statement is highly prejudicial and should be excluded because it could be misinterpreted and it fails to identify V specifically, the court will likely find that its probative value in showing that D committed the murder and that he had a motivation to commit the murder far outweighs the risk of prejudice. Moreover, the information goes to the heart of D's guilt or innocence.

Thus, the evidence will not be excluded on this ground.

Personal Knowledge
See rule above.

Here, Ella was standing by an open window in her kitchen, which was about 20 feet from an open window in D's kitchen. Ella could both see D and W and could hear D tell W that "I just killed the gal who stole my biggest account." Thus, Ella's testimony was based on her percipient observations as she could personally see and hear what was happening in D and W's house.

Thus, this objection will be overruled.

Hearsay

Hearsay is an out-of-court statement that is offered to prove the truth of the matter asserted. Hearsay is inadmissible unless it falls within an exception or is being used for a non-hearsay purpose. Proposition 8 will not apply to admit otherwise inadmissible hearsay as hearsay is an exception to Proposition 8.

Here, Ella's testimony that D told W, "I just killed the gal who stole my biggest account" is offered to show that D was in fact the person who killed V. Thus, it is an out-of-court statement offered to prove the truth of the matter asserted and is only admissible if it falls within an exception.

Party-Opponent Admission

A statement by a party-opponent regarding a relevant fact of the case is admissible over a hearsay objection as it is a California exception from the hearsay prohibition.

Here, the statement that Ella testified about was a statement by D, who is the defendant in the criminal action. This statement is highly relevant to the issues involved in the case because it indicates whether or not D actually committed a murder of V, for which he is being charged.

Thus, this exception would allow the statement to be admitted.

Statement Against Interest

A statement is admissible under an exception if it qualifies as a statement against interest. A statement against interest is a statement of a now unavailable witness that was against the person's proprietary, pecuniary, penal, or social interest when made and that the declarant knew was against his interest when made.

Here, D made the statement to W that "I just killed the gal who stole my biggest account." This statement would be against D's penal interest, because it could subject him to prosecution for murder. Moreover, it could subject him to social ridicule, ostracism and humiliation because he would be labeled as a murderer. D will argue

46

that the statement was not against his interest because it was made to his spouse in reliance on the confidentiality of their marital relationship and thus he did not think that it could be used against him. Moreover, he did not believe at the time it was made that it would subject him to social disgrace as he expected his spouse to maintain the confidentiality of the statement. As D likely did not know that the statement could be used against his interest when it was made, this exception likely would not apply.

A declarant is unavailable if he can claim a privilege against testifying. As D can claim the privilege against self-incrimination under the Fifth Amendment, he would be considered unavailable for the purposes of this exception.

Thus, this exception would not apply because D likely did not know it was against his interest when made.

Spontaneous Statement

A spontaneous statement is a statement made shortly after witnessing a startling event and while the declarant was still under the stress of excitement.

Here, D made his statement to W and said "I just killed the gal..." indicating that he may still have been under the stress of excitement from the murder. Moreover, a murder is likely a startling event, especially when it involved hiding in the bushes and shooting someone at their home and then seeking to avoid detection.

Thus, D's statement might be a spontaneous statement if he was still experiencing the stress of excitement.

Contemporaneous Statement

A contemporaneous statement is a statement made at or near the time of an event that explains or describes the defendant's actions.

Here, D told W, "I just killed the gal who stole my biggest account." Because D specified that he "just" killed a gal, the statement may have been made near the time of the event. Moreover, the statement describes D's own conduct in killing the gal and explains his reasons for that conduct--she "stole my biggest account."

Therefore, provided it was made sufficiently close in time, it may qualify as a contemporaneous statement.

Spousal Communications Privilege

See rule above. In addition, the spousal communications privilege is waived if the privilege is not made in reliance on the intimacy of the marriage. A statement is not made in this reliance, if it is made in the presence of a third person who does not fall within the privilege. If the spouses could not have reasonably foreseen that the communication would be overheard by a third party, then the privilege is not waived and D may prevent Ella from testifying on the basis of the privilege. However, if the spouses made the statement negligently when it could be overheard by a third party, then the privilege has been waived as no reasonable efforts were made to maintain its confidentiality.

Here, D and W had a conversation in their kitchen. No one else was present in the home and D and W were having an intimate conversation as spouses, thus suggesting that the conversation was made in reliance on the intimacy of the marriage. However, D and W had this conversation while the window to their kitchen was open. This window was only 20 feet from a neighbor's window which was also open and D was talking in a sufficiently loud voice such that Ella could overhear the conversation. But, because D and W engaged in a private communication between themselves and they did not know that Ella overheard the communication, they likely were not so negligent as to waive the confidentiality of the communications. D and W could rely on the privacy of their home, even with an open window.

Thus, the spousal communication privilege will prevent this testimony.

(c) Fred

Logical Relevance

Fred's testimony that the day after Vicky was killed he was having lunch and heard that two gangsters had "taken care of the assignment concerning Vicky" is relevant to establish that Dean was not the person who killed Vicky. As whether or not D killed Vicky is the primary issue in the murder trial, this is both highly relevant and in dispute. This objection will be overruled.

Personal Knowledge

Here, Fred was having lunch at a coffee shop when he saw Hit and Gus conversing and overheard the conversation. Thus, Fred had personal knowledge regarding the statements that were made.

This objection will be overruled.

Hearsay

See rule above.

Here, F is offering testimony regarding the statements of both H and G, and both of these statements must fall within a hearsay exception in order to be admitted. These statements are offered to show that F and G committed the murder of Vicky.

G's Statement

Effect on Hearer

D will argue that G's statement asking whether H had "taken care of the assignment concerning Vicky" is not offered to show the truth of that statement, as it was a question, but instead to show its effect on H, who answered the question.

A statement offered to show the effect on the hearer is not hearsay and is admissible over a hearsay objection.

Here, as this question is offered to show the effect on H in answering, it will be admissible.

H's Statement

Although H merely made a gesture by drawing an index finger across his throat, such an action can qualify as hearsay if it is intended to communicate.

Here, H's conduct was done in order to answer G's question regarding whether or not H had "taken care of the assignment concerning Vicky." As this was intended to communicate that H had in fact gotten rid of Vicky, it will qualify as hearsay.

Statement Against Interest

Here, this statement is against H's penal interest as he would be subject to prosecution for murder if he killed Vicky. As H made this statement while at a coffee shop where other people like F were around, H would know that he could be subject to punishment for making it at the time it was made. It is unclear whether H is unavailable and the admissibility will depend on this.

Thus, this is likely admissible testimony.

ANSWER B TO QUESTION 3

People v. Dean

1. Did the court properly allow the prosecution to call Whitney?
Spousal Testimonial Privilege

The California Evidence Code (CEC) contains a spousal privilege. The spousal privilege allows a defendant's spouse to refuse to take the witness stand and testify against his or her spouse. Although Dean's trial is a criminal trial, the CEC makes no distinction between criminal and civil trials--the spouse may refuse to testify against his or her spouse in either civil or criminal trials.

The spouse and defendant must be married during the time of trial. Here, although Whitney had moved out of the house prior to Dean's trial and said the "marriage was over," there is nothing to indicate that Whitney and Dean's marriage was legally dissolved. Thus, Whitney was married to Dean at the time of trial, and therefore can invoke the spousal testimonial privilege.

The spouse--not the defendant--is the holder of the privilege. Thus, even if Dean did not want Whitney to testify against him, Whitney could if she so chose, and so long as the matter she testified to was not otherwise privileged.

Under the CEC, the witness spouse may refuse to take the witness stand completely. Here, although Whitney initially took the stand, intending to testify against Dean, she could have refused to take the stand altogether. The issue is whether Whitney could later invoke the privilege after voluntarily waiving the spousal testimonial privilege.

The CEC does not dictate that a spouse has waived the spousal testimonial privilege once he or she takes the witness stand. Here, Whitney has testified to nothing yet. Thus, although she has taken the witness stand, she is still not otherwise prohibited from invoking the spousal testimonial privilege. Thus, her testimony should not have been compelled.

However, the court did not err in allowing the prosecution to call Whitney to the witness stand because Whitney initially wanted to testify against Dean. Thus, error, if any, was on the court's compelling Whitney to testify, not on the court allowing the prosecution to call Whitney to the witness stand.

2. Did the court properly admit the testimony of Whitney, Ella, and Fred?
Whitney
Logical Relevance

To be admissible, evidence must be relevant. Under the CEC, evidence is relevant if it has any tendency to make the existence of some fact of consequence to the action more or less probable than the absence of such evidence. The CEC further requires that to be relevant, the fact must be in dispute.

Here, Whitney's testimony that she saw mud on Dean's shoes is relevant because it makes a disputed fact--whether Dean was hiding in the bushes outside Vicky's home that rainy night--more probable than the absence of the evidence.

Legal Relevance

Even if logically relevant, the court may exclude evidence if its probative value is substantially outweighed by the risk of unfair prejudice, confusing the issues, or misleading the jury. Here, the probative value of Whitney's testimony is relatively high. Because Whitney is Dean's wife, her testimony tending to inculpate Dean is especially probative. That Dean had mud on his shoes the night of the murder tends to show that Dean might have been hiding in the bushes that night. There is little risk of unfair prejudice because there is nothing to indicate that Whitney's testimony that she saw mud on Dean's shoes will cause the jury to have prejudice against Dean.

Spousal Testimonial Privilege

As discussed above, Whitney should have been able to invoke the spousal testimonial privilege because she is married to Dean at the time of trial and thus may refuse to testify against him. Although she took the stand--which California allows a spouse to refuse to do--Whitney still had the privilege to not testify against Dean.

Confidential Marital Communications Privilege

Whitney may attempt to alternatively invoke the confidential marital communications privilege. Any confidential communication between spouses is privileged and inadmissible. Here, however, Whitney testified as to an observation, not a communication. Whitney merely saw mud on Dean's shoes. Whitney did not testify as to any communication Dean made to her. Thus, the confidential marital communications privilege does not apply.

In conclusion, Whitney's testimony--although relevant--should have been excluded because of the spousal testimonial privilege.

Ella

Logical and Legal Relevance

Ella's testimony that Dean told Whitney "I just killed the gal who stole my biggest account" is extremely relevant. If Dean told Whitney this, it tends to make it more probable that Dean in fact did kill Vicky. The probative value is high, and there is little risk of unfair prejudice as a result of Dean's statement to Whitney.

Hearsay

Ella's testimony may be objected to on the grounds that it is hearsay. Hearsay is an out of court statement being offered to prove the truth of the matter contained therein. Here, Dean's statement is out of court because it was made in his home to his wife. If offered to prove that Dean did kill Vicky, it would be being offered for its truth. Thus, the statement is hearsay by definition.

53

Nonhearsay: Declarant's state of mind

Dean's statement may be offered for the nonhearsay purpose of showing his state of mind. It could be offered to show Dean's intent to kill, rather than the fact that he did kill Vicky. However, if offered only for this purpose, it would be highly prejudicial because it would be very difficult for a jury to not consider the statement as evidence that Dean actually killed Vicky. Thus, it should not likely be admissible solely for this purpose.

Admission of a party/opponent

Alternatively, Dean's statement to Whitney could be offered for its truth if it comes under a hearsay exception. The CEC provides an exception to the hearsay rule for admissions made by parties and offered by an opponent. Here, Dean's statement to Whitney is a statement made by Dean--a party--and offered by the prosecution--an opponent. Thus, although hearsay, Dean's statement may be admissible as an admission--an exception to the CEC's rule against hearsay.

Confidential Marital Communications

However, Dean may seek to exclude his statement to Whitney on the grounds that the statement was a confidential communication between spouses and thus is privileged. Both spouses are holders of the privilege. Here there is a twist because a third person is attempting to testify as to a confidential communication between spouses. Both Dean and Whitney did not know that Ella overheard their conversation. Thus, Dean and Whitney believed Dean's statement to be in confidence. Ella was standing 20 feet away and in the house next door when the statement was made. If Dean and Whitney's belief that the communication was confidential was reasonable, such communication was privileged. Here, it appears that Dean and Whitney's belief that their communication was in confidence was reasonable--notwithstanding the fact that Ella overheard the communication 20 feet away.

The purpose of the confidential marital communications privilege is to foster the confidence of the marital relationship, and to encourage open and honest communication. Here, if Ella is permitted to testify as to Dean's statement if Dean and Whitney reasonably believed their communication was made in confidence, such an allowance would seem to go against the grain of the purpose of the confidential marital communications privilege. Spouses should not have to take every measure to ensure their communications are confidential so as to invoke the benefit of the confidential marital communications privilege. A reasonable belief that the communication is made in confidence should be sufficient. Here, the court should not allow Ella's testimony for this reason.

Logical and Legal Relevance

Fred's testimony that Hit implicitly admitted to killing Vicky is relevant because it makes it more probable that Dean did not kill Vicky. Assuming that the Vicky that Gus was talking about was the same Vicky who died the day before, such evidence would be extremely probative to show that Dean was not the killer, but Hit was.

Hearsay

Hearsay is an out-of-court statement. To be a statement, there must be some assertive words or conduct. Although Gus's question to hit was out of court, it was not a statement because it was not assertive. A question is not an assertion. Thus, Gus's question to Hit whether Hit had taken care of the assignment concerning Vicky was not hearsay.

The issue becomes whether Hit's drawing his index finger across his throat was assertive conduct. Taken in light of the surrounding circumstances, Hit's conduct seems to indicate that Hit acknowledged to Gus that he in fact killed Vicky. To be hearsay, the declarant need not utter actual words. Here, the judge would use his or her discretion in deciding whether Hit's conduct was assertive. The court should hold that the conduct was assertive when taken in context with Gus's immediately preceding question.

Because Hit's assertive conduct was made out of court, and if offered to prove the truth--that Hit did kill Vicky--it is hearsay by definition. Hearsay is inadmissible absent any exception.

Statement against Interest

Dean may argue that Hit's statement was a statement against interest. However, for a statement against interest to be admissible, it must be shown that the declarant is "unavailable" to testify. No such showing has been made, and therefore Hit's statement may not be admitted as a statement against interest.

Admission

Hit's statement cannot come in as an admission because Hit is not a party to the action.

Present Sense Impression/Contemporaneous Statement

Hit's statement may not be admitted under the present sense impression/contemporaneous statement exception because Hit's statement was not made either while killing Vicky or immediately thereafter. Also, Hit was not describing his conduct, he merely made a motion tending to indicate that he killed Vicky. Thus, this exception does not apply.

Confrontation Clause

The Sixth Amendment right to confrontation applies to the states, including California, and provides that criminal defendants shall have the right to be confronted with the witnesses against them. Here, because Dean is offering the out-of-court statement made by Hit, the Sixth Amendment right of confrontation does not apply.

Conclusion

Because Hit's conduct was assertive, given the surrounding circumstances, and because it is only relevant to prove the truth of his statement--that he killed Vicky, and thus inferentially, Dean did not kill Vicky--Hit's statement was hearsay. Because no exception to the rule against hearsay applies, Hit's statement should not have been admitted.

Question 4

Peter responded to an advertisement placed by Della, a dentist, seeking a dental hygienist. After an interview, Della offered Peter the job and said she would either: (1) pay him $50,000 per year; or (2) pay him $40,000 per year and agree to convey to him a parcel of land, worth about $50,000, if he would agree to work for her for three consecutive years. Peter accepted the offer and said, "I'd like to go with the second option, but I would like a commitment for an additional three years after the first three." Della said, "Good, I'd like you to start next week."

After Peter started work, Della handed him a letter she had signed which stated only that he had agreed to work as a dental hygienist at a salary of $40,000 per year.

After Peter had worked for two years and nine months, Della decided that she would sell the parcel of land and not convey it to him. Even though she had always been satisfied with his work, she fired him.

What rights does Peter have and what remedies might he obtain as to employment and the parcel of land? Discuss.

ANSWER A TO QUESTION 4

What rights does Peter have?

The first issue is what law should apply. The UCC applies if the contract is for sale of goods. The common law applies if in all other circumstances, including a contract for services or land. In this case, there is an employment contract that contemplates the payment of a salary and a land conveyance in exchange for services. Thus, the common law applies to this contract.

The second issue is whether there is a valid contract. A valid contract requires offer, acceptance, and consideration. An offer exists if the offeror offers the offeree a deal and signals that acceptance will conclude the deal. An acceptance occurs if the offeree agrees to the terms of the offeror and gives the offeree notice of his assent. Consideration exists if there is a bargained-for exchange and legal detriment (which involves perform [SIC] in a way that one is not legally required to perform). Acceptance only exists if the offeree consents to the exact terms of the offeror, also known as the mirror image rule. If the offeree attempts to change any terms of the offer, then there is an effective rejection and counteroffer. Della advertised for a dental hygienist. Advertisements are not usually considered offers and Della's advertisement did not indicate that anyone who responded would be hired. The need to conduct an interview suggests that Della's advertisement was an invitation to make an offer, not an actually offer. Della interviewed Peter and offered him a job. She gave him a choice of being paid $50,000 per year, or being paid $40,000 per year and the conveyance of a $50,000 parcel of land at the completion of three years of work. This might have been an offer because it signaled to Peter that the deal would be complete if he chose either option. However, it would more likely be considered preliminary negotiations since Peter could still choose which option he preferred. Peter said, "I'd like to go with the second option..." If there was an offer, and he had left his statement at this, then this would constitute acceptance because it gave Della notice that he was accepting her offer. However, Peter attempted to modify the terms of the deal by adding a commitment for an additional three years after the first three years. Thus, Peter's attempted acceptance was ineffective because it altered the terms of Della's offer and does not meet the mirror image rule. Rather, Peter effectively made a counteroffer to Della (or an offer if Della's original options were considered preliminary negotiations). Della accepted Peter's counteroffer when she said, "Good, I'd like you to start next week." The exchange of six years of dental hygienist services for a $50,000 parcel of land and a $40,000 per year salary constitutes consideration. Because there was an offer, an acceptance, and consideration, there is a valid contract.

The third issue is whether the statute of frauds makes the service or land contract unenforceable. The statute of frauds requires some contracts to be in a writing signed by the party against whom enforcement is sought. Contracts for land and contracts that cannot be completed within a year are both included within the statute of frauds. Contracts for land must adequately identify the parties and the parcel of land to be conveyed. The contract between Della and Peter was for six years of employment. Peter could not complete his performance of six years of services within one year, thus this contract falls within the statute of frauds. The contract between Della and Peter also contemplated the conveyance of an interest in land. Della did sign a contract with Peter, but the contract only specified that Peter agreed to work as a dental hygienist for a salary of $40,000 per year. The conveyance of land was not considered within the signed contract, nor was the length of the term of employment. Thus, the contract Della signed cannot be used to overcome the statute of frauds. The employment contract for a term of years and the land conveyance are both unenforceable under the statute of frauds.

The fourth issue is whether Peter can overcome the Statute of Frauds defense via the doctrine of part performance or equitable estoppel. Part performance in a land conveyance requires that the party who seeks to enforce the contract must have engaged in partial performance, which is usually evidenced by possession or payment of the purchase price. Equitable estoppel requires that the party who seeks to enforce the contract show that there was a promise and that the party reasonably relied upon that promise to their detriment. It will probably be difficult for Peter to show partial performance since he has not taken possession of the land or paid the full purchase price. He might be able to argue that he has "paid" a substantial portion of the purchase price since he worked for two years and nine months, which is the equivalent of 75% of the service he was to perform before receiving the land. However, equitable estoppel is probably a better argument for him to make. The fact that Della offered Peter two options suggests that $40,000 was less than the market rate for dental hygienists. Peter chose the option that gave him less yearly salary in reliance on Della's promise that he would be employed for six years and would receive a $50,000 parcel of land. He received less salary than he otherwise would have, so his reliance was detrimental. Peter may be able to overcome Della's Statute of Frauds defense under the doctrine of equitable estoppel.

The fifth issue is whether there was a breach of contract. A breach occurs when one party fails to perform as obligated under the express and implied conditions in the contract. Assuming that the court finds a valid and enforceable contract, then Della committed a breach when she fired Peter before the six years were complete. She also committed an anticipatory repudiation when she decided to sell the land instead of convey the land to him. She also potentially breached her implied duty of good faith by firing Peter when she was satisfied with his work.

What remedies might Peter obtain?

The first issue is whether Peter can receive expectation damages. The general measure of damages in a contracts case attempts to put the plaintiff into the position he would have been in if the contract had been fully performed. A plaintiff does have a duty to mitigate, which requires that he make a reasonable effort to find similar employment. He does not have to settle for lesser employment or move to a distant location to find employment. Assuming that the court finds there was an employment contract for six years, the court would award three years and three months worth of the $40,000 per year salary if Peter cannot find similar employment. If Peter can find similar employment, the reward will be reduced based on whatever his new salary is. Assuming that the court finds there was a contract to convey land, Peter could sue for the value of the land, which was $50,000. If the court finds that there was an employment contract, but no contract to convey land, then Peter might be able to receive more than the $40,000 per year salary award if he can show that he took a reduced salary in reliance on the promise that he would receive a land conveyance.

The second issue is whether Peter can receive restitutionary damages. Restitutionary damages are only awarded when a benefit has been bestowed and it would unjustly enrich the other party if they are not required to pay for that benefit. A plaintiff cannot receive restitutionary remedies if they receive expectation damages. Restitutionary damages would probably not be Peter's best option. However, Peter might be able to receive the difference between his salary and the market rate salary for a dental hygienist if he can show that he took the lower salary in reliance on the promise to receive land.

The third issue is whether Peter can receive specific performance. Specific performance is awarded when there is a definite and certain contract, an inadequate legal remedy, enforcement of specific performance is feasible for the court, and there is mutuality. The party attempting to avoid specific performance can do so by raising various defenses, such as laches or unclean hands. Assuming Peter overcomes the statute of fraud objections, Peter will not be able to seek specific performance for the employment contract. Attempting to enforce an employment contract, which is a contract for personal services, is not feasible for the court. Personal service and employment contracts require individuals to work together in a cooperative environment; it is not feasible for the court to monitor the relationship between the parties. Peter probably will not be able to seek specific performance for the land contract. There was a definite and certain contract to convey a parcel of land worth $50,000, though there may be some issues with this element if it is not clear which parcel of land Della intended to convey. Land is considered unique, so a legal remedy of $50,000 would be inadequate. It would be feasible for the court to enforce the specific performance. Under the common law doctrine of mutuality, both parties must have been able to request specific performance. In this case, Della could not have sought specific performance if Peter breached. However, under the modern theory, the requirement for mutuality is met if one party can sufficiently assure performance. The court would have to decide if the two years and nine months was enough to constitute full performance, but this is only 75% of the total performance required. Peter may be willing to work the remaining three months, but the court cannot require him to do it. Thus, there is no mutuality and Peter cannot successfully obtain specific performance.

ANSWER B TO QUESTION 4

What Rights Does Peter Have as to Employment and the Parcel of Land

I. The Contract, if Valid, Is Governed By Common Law

The issue is what law governs the contract, if valid, between Peter (P) and Della (D). The UCC governs contracts involving the sale of goods. Contracts which are for services or are land contracts are governed by the common law. Here, P and D are contracting for employment and possibly land. This is a contract for services and land and therefore the contract is governed by common law principles.

II. There is Likely a Valid Contract Between Peter and Della

The issue is whether Peter and Della actually entered into a valid contract. For a contract to be valid, it must contain offer, acceptance, and consideration. An offer is an outward manifestation by the offeror that creates the power of acceptance in the offeree. An advertisement can be a valid offer is it is made to a particular person, outlines the specific details of the offer, and presents the recipient of the advertisement with instructions as to how acceptance can be made. Acceptance is an outward manifestation by the offeree that he accepts the terms of the offeror. Acceptance must mirror the terms of the offer. If acceptance does not mirror the terms of the offer or, in itself, alters the terms of the offer, it is a counteroffer and effectively rejects the original offer. However, a mere inquiry is not a counteroffer. Consideration is a bargained-for legal detriment. (i.e., A works for B in exchange for a salary).

Here, P responded to an advertisement from D, a dentist, who was seeking a dental hygienist. The advertisement was not a valid offer because there are no facts that it was sent directly to P, there are no facts that it contained the details of any potential employment contract, and there are not facts that it told P how he could accept. However, when D interviewed P, she presented him with a valid offer to be her hygienist for three years in exchange for either (1) working for $50,000 per year; or (2) working for $40,000 per year and she would agree to convey to him a parcel of land, worth about $50,000. When P accepted, he said "I'd like to go with the second option, but I would like a commitment for an additional three years after the first three." This acceptance by P does not mirror the terms of the offer by D and therefore acts as both a rejection of the offer and a counteroffer. Della said, "Good, I'd like you to start next week."

Peter will argue that Della's comment of "Good, I'd like you to start next week," is her acceptance of his counteroffer. He will argue that the terms of the deal are that he works for Della for 6 years at $40,000 per year and is conveyed the parcel of land after the first three years. When P started to work and D handed him the letter stating only that he had agreed to work as a hygienist for $40,000 per year, P will argue that this letter is merely a documentation of the salary he is to receive and nothing more.

In conclusion, Peter's counteroffer is the controlling offer and D accepted it by saying, "Good, I'd like you to start next week." The consideration is that Peter work for 6 years at $40,000 and will receive the parcel of land at the completion of the first three years. The consideration is valid. There is likely a valid contract between P and D.

III. The Letter D Presented to P Is An Invalid Modification

The issue is whether the letter D presented to P is an invalid modification. Under the Common Law, a modification to a contract must be supported by consideration. The pre-existing duty rule prohibits the modification of any contractual duties which have been agreed to absent consideration because the party is attempting to modify something that he/she is currently obligated to do.

Here, D attempted to modify the existing when she presented P with a letter, which she signed, documenting P would work as a dental hygienist for $40,000 and no other elements of the deal between P and D were documented. There was no consideration paid by D to P to enforce this modification and it is invalid.

In conclusion, the modification is invalid because D is obligated to have P work for 6 years at $40,000 and convey a piece of land to him after 3 years of work. To reduce her obligations to only paying him $40,000 per year without consideration is in violation of the pre-existing duty rule.

IV. <u>Della Can Assert the Defense of Statute of Frauds (SOF)</u>

The issue is whether D can assert a SOF defense. The SOF requires that certain contracts be in writing. The categories are contracts regarding marriage, contracts which cannot be performed within one year, land sale contracts, executor agreements, guarantees or suretyships, and contracts for the sale of goods for over $500. A contract which cannot be performed within one year is determined at the time of the contract execution and is measured by whether there is any possibility performance can be completed within one year. The writing that will satisfy the SOF must contain the essential terms of the contract and be signed by the party to be charged.

Here, P's contract is for 6 years, or, at the least, 3 years, and is clearly not performable within one year. This contract is subject to the statute of frauds. The parties did not sign a written contract for P's services to D. Further, part of the deal is a land conveyance which is also subject to the SOF. Neither of those terms were ever written down and D can assert that the contract fails under the SOF. Peter will argue that the letter D gave to him after he started working is a writing confirming their contract because it says he gets paid $40,000 and it is signed by D. However, this is not the same contract to which they agreed.

In conclusion, it is likely that D can assert a valid SOF defense because the ` contract was not in a writing which comports with the requirements of the SOF.

V. P Can Assert The Defense of Estoppel and Likely Partial Performance to the SOF Requirements.

The issue is whether P can assert the defenses of estoppel or part performance to the SOF requirements. As stated above certain writings are subject to the SOF. There are four defenses to the enforcement of the SOF: (1) Partial or Full Performance, (2) Estoppel, (3) Judicial Acknowledgement of Contract, and (4) Merchant's Confirmation Memo. There has been no acknowledgement in a judicial proceeding and the merchant's confirmatory memo is only for UCC contracts with a merchant, so neither apply. However, Partial or Full Performance and Estoppel may apply.

Partial or Full Performance

A party may not comply with the requirements of the SOF if he partially or fully performs his contract and the other party accepts the benefits of the performance. Here, P worked for D for 2 years and 9 months. At the very least, D was under the impression that P was going to be working for her for 3 years, even though the final accepted offer was likely for 6. There are no facts which say she failed to pay him so she very likely was performing her obligations under the contract. She was accepting his benefit of being a hygienist in exchange for her payment. Therefore, under the doctrine of part performance, P has a meritorious defense to the requirments of the SOF.

Equitable Estoppel

A party may not comply with the requirements of the SOF if he can assert a defense of estoppel. Equitable estoppel occurs when a party says or does something that foreseeably creates action in another person, the other person relies on the party's previous statement or action, and it would be unjustly prejudicial to the relying party. Here, P has fully relied on Ds statement of acceptance to his counteroffer. He began working for her and has been working for her for almost 3 years. D has reason to know that he was working for her based on their discussions of the $40,000 and land conveyance. P may not have started working for D without the provisions agreed to in his counteroffer and therefore it would be unfairly prejudicial not to enforce his contract.

In conclusion, P has a likely defense of partial or full performance ot the SOF and may have a mertitorious defense of Estoppel.

VI. If A Valid Contract Exists, It is A Contract For Term and Not an At-Will Contract

The issue is whether the contract is a contract for term or an at-will contract. In a contract for term, an employee has a property right in the job and may not be terminated without cause. Conversely, an at-will contract allows the employer or employee to terminate employment for good cause, bad cause, or no cause.

Here, P will argue that this is a contract for terms because the terms of his counteroffer were that he worked for D for 6 years. Further, he will argue that even if her original job offer is controlling, that offer was for a 3 year term. Either way, it is not an at-will employment. Since it was not at will, she was not able to fire him because she had always been happy with his work. Della will argue that her letter modifying the contract has no language regarding term and therefore it is an at-will employment and she can fire him for any reason.

In conclusion, this is a contract for term and P may not be fired absent cause.

In conclusion, P and D have a valid contract for 6 years at $40,000 per year. Further, D is obligated by the contract to convey P the parcel of land upon completion of his 3rd year. Peter has a right to seek remedies for breach of contract.

What Remedies Can Peter Seek

VII. Peter May Seek Expectation Damages and Reliance Damages

The issue is whether Peter may seek expectation damages and reliance damages for his contract with Della. Legal remedies are available if the plaintiff can clearly estimate the damages incurred with specificity. Legal damages are in three categories, expectation, reliance, and restitution. Expectation damages place the plaintiff in the position he would have been in had the breaching party performed the contract in full. Reliance damages place the plaintiff in the place he would have been had the contract not existed. Restitution damages reimburse the plaintiff for any benefit conferred on the defendant. A plaintiff always has the duty to mitigate damages and, in the employment context, the duty to to find other employment. The plaintiff is not required to find any job, but rather a job comparable to the job that has been taken. If a plaintiff cannot find replacement employment, a good faith effort must take place to find employment.

Here, P will argue that he should get his expectation, or benefit of the bargain damages, from the contract including any incidental and consequential damages that are reasonably foreseeable from D's breach.. He can easily estimate them because he was due 3 years and 3 months salary and the parcel of land. He had a right to those damages because he was under a contract for which he was improperly fired. These damages will place him in the position he would have been in had he not been fired and the contract been performed. However, he has a duty to find alternative employment and there are no facts which say he has looked for or obtained any further employment. Also, there are no facts that say he has acted in bad faith which would negate the award of damages. If and when he does, his salary from that employment can be applied against his damages from D. There are no facts indicating any incidental and consequential damages.

Also, if P spent any money in reliance on his contract with D, he may recover those costs that are reasonable and foreseeable. Any money that he spent in reliance on the contract with D is obtainable.

In conclusion, he can obtain expectation and reliance damages from D less his duty to mitigate by finding other, comparable employment.

VIII. Peter May Seek Specific Performance of the Land Contract, But Not the Services Contract

The issue is whether Peter can seek specific performance of the land contract. Specific performance is available when the contract has definite and certain terms, there is an inadequate legal remedy, the court can correctly adjudicate, there is mutuality between the parties and there are no defenses. Inadequate legal remedy applies when you are dealing with land or unique items. Mutuality has been relaxed and no longer requires that the parties must each be able to get specific performance. Just that the party is ready and willing to perform. Specific performance will not be applied to a services contract because it is difficult to enforce and can abridge certain constitutional provisions against servitude.

Here, the land at issue is unique and is a definite term of the contract. Money damages will not suffice. Peter contracted and performed for the piece of land. The judge can properly adjudicate the matter. However, Peter likely may not seek specific performance of the services contract.

In conclusion, P may seek specific performance of the land contract but not the services contract.

Question 5

In 2004, Mae, a widow, executed a valid will, intentionally leaving out her daughter, Dot, and giving 50 per cent of her estate to her son, Sam, and 50 per cent to Church.

In 2008, after a serious disagreement with Sam, Mae announced that she was revoking her will, and then tore it in half in the presence of both Sam and Dot.

In 2010, after repeated requests by Sam, Mae handwrote and signed a document declaring that she was thereby reviving her will. She attached all of the torn pages of the will to the document. At the time she signed the document, she was entirely dependent on Sam for food and shelter and companionship, and had not been allowed by Sam to see or speak to anyone for months. By this time, Church had gone out of existence.

In 2011, Mae died. Her sole survivors are Dot and Sam.

What rights, if any, do Dot and Sam have in Mae's estate? Discuss.

Answer according to California law

ANSWER A TO QUESTION 5

Sam's Rights

In 2004, Mae executed a valid will that left 50% of her estate to her son, Sam, and 50% of her estate to Church.

Revocation of 2004 Will

A will can be revoked by physical act. This requires that the testator tear, cancel, obliterate, or destroy the will with the contemporaneous intent to revoke it. Here, in 2008, Mae had a disagreement with Sam and announced that she was revoking her will as she tore the will in half, in the presence of both Sam and Dot. Because she announced that she was revoking the will, that shows that she had an intent to revoke it. Additionally, she got into a fight with Sam prior to this, and Sam was to take 50% of her estate under that will. That further evidences that she intended to revoke the will. She tore the will in half, which is a sufficient physical act. Thus, her actions in 2008 are sufficient to count as a revocation by physical act. At this point in 2008, because Mae revoked her only will, she does not have a testamentary instrument.

Revival in 2010

Holograph

A holographic will is one that is signed by the testator and all of the material terms are in the testator's handwriting. Material terms are the beneficiaries and the gifts. In 2010, Mae handwrote and signed a document that stated she was reviving her will. Although it is signed by Mae and in her handwriting, the material terms are not in her handwriting because they are referenced. Thus, this will only be a valid holograph if the 2004 will can be incorporated into the 2010 handwritten note because the 2004 will contains the material terms.

Incorporation of the 2004 Will

A document will be incorporated as part of the will if it was physically present at the time the will was executed and there was a simultaneous intent that the document be a part of the will. Here, it seems that the torn pieces of the 2004 will were physically present when Mae wrote the holograph because there are no facts suggesting she had to go anywhere to get it; rather the facts seem to suggest that she wrote the holograph and attached the torn pages in one sitting. Thus, it can be presumed that the prior will was physically present when she wrote the holograph.

Furthermore, Mae had intent to incorporate the prior will because she physically attached the torn pages of the will to the holograph document. This is sufficient to prove her intent to incorporate.

Because the prior will was physically present and was intended to be a part of the holograph, it will be revived in accordance with Mae's intent.

Incorporation by Reference

A writing can be incorporated by reference into a will if (1) there is a writing, (2) it existed at the time of the will's execution, (3) it is specifically referenced in the will, and (4) the testator had the intent to incorporate the writing.

Here, the 2004 will was in writing because it was valid at the time it was executed, so it must have been in writing to be valid. It existed at the time of the will's execution because Mae still had the torn pages. It is irrelevant that at that time it was not a valid testamentary document, so long as it physically existed. It was specifically referenced within the 2010 will because she stated that she wanted to revive her will, and she only had one prior will that had been revoked. Furthermore, she attached the torn pages to the 2010 will, so it is evident that she is talking about the 2004 will. Because the first three elements are satisfied, there is a presumption that Mae had the intent to incorporate the 2004 will into the 2010 holograph.

Independently Significant Fact

A fact is independently significant if it would have existed regardless of the testamentary document being executed. Here, the 2004 will would have existed regardless of the 2010 holograph because it was written prior to the 2010 holograph. Even if Mae had never written the 2010 will, the 2004 will would have existed, regardless of the fact that she revoked it. The torn pieces still remained. Thus, the 2004 will is independently significant.

Validity of 2010 Will: Undue Influence

Dot, who takes nothing under the revived will, will argue that the 2010 will was the product of undue influence, and is therefore invalid, leaving Mae without a testamentary instrument. There are three types of undue influence recognized in California: the prima facie case, case law undue influence, or statutory undue influence.

Prima Facie Case

Under the prima facie case, undue influence can be shown if the testator was susceptible to undue influence, if there was an opportunity to influence her, if there was action taken to cause undue influence, and there was an unnatural disposition of the estate because of the undue influence.

Here, Dot will argue that Mae was susceptible to undue influence by Sam because she was entirely dependent on Sam for food, shelter, and companionship. Thus, she was susceptible to doing what Sam wanted her to do. Dot will argue that Sam had the opportunity to influence Mae because she was so dependent on him, Mae felt that if she did not do what he wanted, she would have been left without food, shelter, or companionship. There was active participation by Sam because he had repeatedly requested that Mae revive the 2004 [will] and would not allow Mae to see or speak to anyone for months. Finally, Dot will argue that the gift in the 2004 will was unnatural because it did not provide for her, Dot, Mae's own daughter. Sam will argue, on the other hand, that the gift revived by the 2010 will was not unnatural because it was a will that was validly executed in 2004. There was nothing unnatural about it in 2004, and there is nothing unnatural about it now. Furthermore, Mae intentionally left Dot out of the will in 2004, so it was not unnatural to be left out now. Finally, Sam will argue that Mae was not susceptible to any undue influence by him; rather he was just taking care of his aging mother.

Ultimately, the court will probably side with Sam, that there was not an unnatural disposition of Mae's property in the 2010 instrument because it was merely the revival of a valid gift that she had already devised, despite the fact that she later revoked it. Thus, the will will not be found invalid because of prima facie undue influence.

Case Law Undue Influence

Under case law undue influence, a gift or a will is invalid if there was a confidential relationship between the testator and the person accused of having undue influence, if there was active participation by the person causing the undue influence, and if there was an unnatural gift because of the undue influence. Here, there is a confidential relationship between Sam and Mae because Sam is Mae's son and he is solely responsible for taking care of her. Mae is entirely dependent on Sam, so there is a confidential relationship.

See above for arguments regarding active participation by Sam and the fact that the gift was not an unnatural disposition of property.

Because the revival of the 2004 will by the 2010 will was not an unnatural disposition of property, discussed above, there will be no undue influence.

Statutory Undue Influence

Under the California Probate Code, undue influence is presumed if the drafter of the will is also the beneficiary of the will. Here, Mae handwrote the 2010 holograph and attached the torn pages to that will herself. Thus, no one else drafted the will. The fact that she did so at the repeated requests of Sam does not change the fact that he did not draft the will leaving a gift to himself. Even if he did, there is an exception to this general rule that if the drafter is also a relative of the testator, there is not going to be a presumption of undue influence. Thus, there is no statutory undue influence.

Disposition re: Sam

If the court finds that there is no undue influence, the court will dispose of Mae's estate in accordance with the 2010 will, which incorporates the 2004 will. Under that document, Sam is entitled to 50% of Mae's estate, and Church is entitled to the other 50%.

Church: Lapse of Gift

Church was no longer in existence in 2010, when Mae executed her will. Thus, her gift of 50% of the estate will lapse because Church does not exist and is not there to take its gift.

Anti-Lapse?

California has an anti-lapse statute, which allows for the issue of a kindred beneficiary to take, despite the fact that he or she may have predeceased the testator. Here, however, Church is not kindred, or blood-related, to Mae, nor does it leave issue because it is an entity. Thus, anti-lapse will not apply to Church's gift of 50%.

Remaining 50%: Intestacy

Because the gift of 50% of Mae's estate to Church will lapse, the will does not provide for the distribution of that property. Thus, the remaining 50% of Mae's estate will pass through intestacy.

Mae was a widow when she died, so she did not leave a surviving spouse. She was survived solely by Dot and Sam, her children. Under the rules of intestacy, if a decedent dies without a will or without full disposition of property by a will, the property will go to the surviving issue, per capita. Under California Probate Code section 240, you go to the first generation with living issue and divide the estate equally among bloodlines with someone living. Here, Sam and Dot are both living, and they are in the first generation. Thus, they will each take 50% of the remaining estate - in other words, they will get 25% of Mae's estate each.

Dot's Rights

Dot was intentionally left out of the 2004 will, which later was revoked and then incorporated into the 2010 will. Thus, under Mae's will, Dot stands to take nothing (with the exception of her 25% intestate share due to the lapse of Church's gift).

Pretermitted Child

Dot will argue that she is a pretermitted child. A pretermitted child is one that was not born or known about at the time the testamentary instrument was executed. Pretermitted children are entitled to their intestate share of the entire estate. Thus, if Dot is pretermitted, she will be entitled to 50% of Mae's estate because Mae's estate would be split 50/50 between her two children in intestacy.

Here, Dot is not a pretermitted child because she was alive in 2004 when Mae executed the will. Furthermore, Mae intentionally left her out of the 2004 will and she revived that will, with the intent that it go back into effect. Therefore, Dot will not be construed as a pretermitted child.

Distribution of Mae's Estate

If Dot is able to persuade the court that there was undue influence by Sam, his gift will be invalidated because of the undue influence. If Sam's gift is invalid and Church's gift lapse, that would mean Mae's entire estate would be distributed through intestacy. In this case, Dot and Sam, as the sole surviving children, would be entitled to 50% each.

However, as discussed above, the court is unlikely to find that undue influence will invalidate Sam's gift because it was not unnatural. Therefore, Sam will still be entitled to his 50% under the will. Because Church's gift lapsed, however, the remaining 50% will be distributed under intestacy, with 25% going to each Sam and Dot. Thus, the most likely distribution of Mae's estate results with Sam taking 75% of the estate, and Dot taking 25%.

ANSWER B TO QUESTION 5

2004 - Valid Will

The facts here indicate that Mae executed a valid will in 2004 in which she intentionally omitted D, and split her estate 50/50 between S and the Church.

2008 - Revocation

A will can be revoked by physical act or subsequent testamentary documents. When revoking by physical act, testator, or someone under testator's direction must burn, tear, destroy, or cancel the will. The testator must have the intent to revoke at the same time. Here, in 2008, after a disagreement with S, M announced that she was revoking her will, thereby indicating an intent to revoke, and then she tore it in half, fulfilling the necessary physical act to revoke. Because she tore the entire will in half, there is an indication that she intended to revoke the entire will, not just a part of it.

As such, Mae effectively revoked her 2008 will.

2010 - Revival

A will can only be revived if it was revoked by a subsequent testamentary instrument, which was then later revoked by physical act or another testamentary instrument. Revival re-effectuates an earlier will. Here, Mae's 2004 will was revoked by physical act, not by testamentary instrument, so it cannot be revived by a document. Had this will been revoked by a later instrument, S could argue that the first will was revived because his mother executed a holographic codicil that explicitly stated that she intended the earlier will be back in effect, and it would have been effective as of the date of the codicil.

However, a will revoked by physical act cannot be revived.

2010 - Holographic Will

S could argue that in 2010, his mother executed a holographic will. A valid holographic will requires that all material terms of the will be in the testator's handwriting, and it be signed by her. Here, Mae wrote that she was reviving her will and she signed the document. He could argue that even though this was not a valid revival, as discussed above, it was a new will because testamentary intent can be inferred from her statement that she wished to revive the earlier will, and she had signed and handwritten this new will. Therefore, Sam may be able to argue that this was a new, valid holographic will.

To establish the terms of the will, he could look to integration, and incorporation.

Integration

A writing that is present at the time of the execution of a will, and is intended to be a part of that will, is deemed to have been integrated into the will and is probated. An intent to make it a part of the will can be established by it being attached to the will. Here, S could argue that even though the previous will had been revoked, the pieces of it were attached to the holographic will that his mother executed, and therefore, it was integrated into the new will and should be probated. There is no requirement that the attached documents be valid on their own. Therefore, Sam may be successful in arguing that his mother's former will was integrated into the holographic will.

Incorporation by reference

A writing, whether valid or not, can also be incorporated by reference if it is in existence at the time of the execution of the will, it is identified in the will, and there is an intent to incorporate it. Sam could again argue that if his mother's will was not integrated, it was incorporated by reference because she states in the new will that she is reviving her former will, which indicates that she intended to incorporate it, and it is clearly referenced in the new will. He can also argue that even though it was in two pieces, it was still in existence at the time of the execution of this will. Thus, it was incorporated by reference.

Undue Influence

Courts are unwilling to probate wills or terms of a will that are procured by undue influence. Undue influence is when the testator's freewill is overcome. There are two types of undue influence that the court may find were at play when Mae wrote the document attempting to revive her former will: prima facie undue influence and undue influence based on case law.

Prima facie

To establish a prima facie case of undue influence, a party contesting the will, which in this case could be D because she receives nothing under her mother's initial will, would have to show her mother's susceptibility to be influenced, her brother's opportunity to influence Mae, S's active participation in influence, and an unnatural result.

Susceptibility

Mae must have been in a vulnerable position in which her freewill could have been overcome. In this case, she was completely dependent on S for her basic necessities in life, such as food, shelter and companionship. Therefore, she was very likely susceptible to having her freewill overcome by Sam.

Opportunity

S must also have had the opportunity to overcome Mae's freewill. In this case, Sam did not allow Mae to see or speak to anyone for months, and his mother completely relied upon him. Therefore, because he was her only source of companionship, he had the opportunity to influence her.

Active participation

S must have actively influenced his mother. Here, he made repeated requests to her to revive her former will, and it was only after these repeated requests that she did so. Therefore, he actively participated.

An unnatural disposition

Proving an unnatural disposition may be difficult for D because the original will devised half of Mae's property to S and that's also what the new will would do. Furthermore, if Mae died intestate, he would still receive half of her property because she only left behind two issues. However, because it is clear that Mae intended to tear up her old will, and that this second document was only the result of S's pressure on her, it may be possible for find undue influence.

Case law

Under the case law method of proving undue influence, there has to be a special relationship between the influencer and the testator, active participation and an unnatural result. Here, the special relationship can be established through the familial bond, as S was Mae's son, and she was completely dependent on him to take care of her. See above for the other two elements.

As a result, if the court were to find that there was undue influence, it would likely refuse to probate the second will because the entire thing was obtained by such an influence. On the other hand, because the disposition wasn't entirely unnatural, it may not find undue influence, in which case it would be a valid will that could be probated.

Gift to the Church

In order to obtain a gift under the will, one must be in existence at the time of testator's death. The church here was no longer in existence when Mae died. Under California's lapse provisions, the gift to the church would lapse and fall into the either the residuary clause of the testator's will, and if there wasn't one, then it would pass under intestacy. The gift cannot be saved under the antilapse provisions because only kindred who leave behind issue can benefit from that provision.

As such, if there was a valid will, the gift to the church would lapse, and as there is no residuary clause, it would pass under intestacy.

Dot's Rights
Omitted Child

Dot could claim that she was an omitted child because she was not provided for in any of Mae's wills. However, to be an omitted child, all testamentary documents must have been executed prior to the birth of the child. Here, the facts clearly indicate that D was alive when Mae executed her will in 2004, and then also again in 2010 if that is deemed to be a valid will, and thus she was not an omitted child. Furthermore, Mae intentionally left D out.

Intestacy Share

D's intestacy share will depend on whether the holographic will by Mae is considered valid or invalid.

If the will is valid, 50% of her estate would pass under the will to S. The other 50% that was to go to the church would have lapsed, as would pass under intestate distribution as there is no document governing the disposition of that property.

Under the default rules for intestate distribution, when there is no surviving spouse, which there isn't here because Mae was a widow, distribution to issue is on a "per capita" basis. Each of Mae's children would get an equal share of the intestate property. As Mae has two children, and 50% of her estate is passing by intestacy, D would get 25% of the total estate.

If on the other hand, the will is invalid, then all of Mae's estate would pass by intestacy. Just as above, the property would be distributed equally between her two children, and D would therefore get 50% of the estate.

Sam's Rights

Sam's rights to distribution will depend on whether the will is deemed invalid because of his undue influence or because it was not a proper holographic will.

If the will is valid, S is entitled to receive 50% of Mae's estate under the will. The other 50% that would not pass to the church because it is no longer in existence would pass through intestacy because of a lack of a residuary clause. Under intestacy, as discussed above for D, Sam would receive 50% of the property that passes in such a manner, which would result in a 25% share of the total estate. Overall, if the will is deemed valid, Sam would receive 75% of Mae's estate.

If the will is not valid, then all of Mae's property would pass under intestacy, and S would receive half just the same as D above. Therefore, he would get 50% of Mae's estate.

Overall

Overall, the rights of D and S depend on whether the court finds that Mae had a valid will at the time of her death. If there was a valid will, S would receive 75% of his mother's estate, and D would receive 25%. If there was no valid will, then each S and D would receive a 50% share.

Question 6

Dan worked at a church. One day a woman came to the church, told Dan she wanted to donate some property to the church, and handed him an old book and a handgun.

Dan had originally intended to deliver both the book and the gun to the church's administrators, but he changed his mind and delivered only the book. He put the gun on the front seat of his car.

The next day, as he was driving, Dan was stopped by a police officer at a sobriety checkpoint at which officers stopped all cars and asked their drivers to exit briefly before going on their way. The police officer explained the procedure and asked, "Would you please exit the vehicle?"

Believing he had no choice, Dan said, "Okay."

After Dan got out of his car, the police officer observed the gun on the front seat and asked Dan if he was the owner. Dan answered, "No. I stole the gun. But I was planning to give it back."

Dan is charged with theft and moves to suppress the gun and his statement to the police officer under the Fourth Amendment to the United States Constitution and Miranda v. Arizona.

1. Is Dan likely to prevail on his motion? Discuss.

2. If Dan does not prevail on his motion, is he likely to be convicted at trial? Discuss.

ANSWER A TO QUESTION 6

1. **Is Dan ("D") likely to prevail on his motion?**

A. On Fourth Amendment Grounds. The Fourth Amendment protects the citizenry from unreasonable searches and seizures by the government. Thus violations require government action. They also require that the search or seizure be unreasonable, something that may be an issue for D. A search is a violation of a reasonable expectation of property; a seizure is an instance in which a person does not feel "free to leave" based on governmental presence. Generally, for a search to be reasonable, there must be a warrant. A warrant is granted by a neutral judge and must be based on articulable facts shown in an affidavit and must be reasonable and particular in terms of scope and time. In this case, there was no warrant to search D's car or to seize D. Thus, the search and seizure is presumptively unreasonable, subject to certain exceptions. One important exception is the checkpoint search; another such exception is consent. As an initial matter, a person must have standing to challenge the search. Because Dan was driving his own car, he will have standing.

i) The Checkpoint Search: Warrantless, even suspicionless, road checkpoints have been upheld by the Supreme Court under certain circumstances. First, the search must be supported by the justification of highway safety - including prevention of DUI, etc. Second, the checkpoints must be administered in such a way that officer discretion is very limited. This means that an officer must go through a protocol driven method of stopping the cars - i.e., either every car, or one of every ten cars, etc. The officer may not stop whatever car he subjectively thinks looks criminal. Third, the search must be reasonable in scope - it must not exceed the degree necessary to check for whatever the search is aimed at.

Here, it does appear that the checkpoint search is aimed at a valid justification - a sobriety checkpoint. This has been expressly held as constitutional by the Supreme Court. However, there are some other issues. For one, all cars are being stopped. While this is not presumptively unreasonable, it will be an issue, as it basically allows a policeman to stop and seize every single person driving down the expressway. Secondly, the police required D to step out of his car. Under Supreme Court precedent, police only have been allowed to stop people. If sobriety or another criminal violation seem likely, then the people can be asked to exit their car. Because of the stopping of every car, and the demand that the drivers exit the car, this may be found to be an unreasonably long stop than what is necessary to meet the highway safety justification.

Conclusion: There is a chance that this checkpoint too far exceeds permissible protocol based on Supreme Court precedent. However, it is a close call. I will consider this to be a reasonable and permissible warrantless search, though the court may be convinced otherwise.

ii) Consent to Search: A person may validly waive his right to be free from unreasonable search and seizure by giving consent. Because it is likely that the stop and seizure was permissible up until the time that D was removed from his car, his consent to get out of the car would completely remove any potential objection to the search and seizure. The question will be whether the consent was freely and voluntarily given. Courts have found that when police attempt to search a person's house on the basis of consent, they do not have to tell that person that he or she has the right to refuse consent. This does not remove the "voluntary" aspect of consent. Here, Dan subjectively thought that he had no choice, but he still consented to getting out of the car. Assuming that the court would apply the consent rule used in home searches to a car search, this consent should be found to be voluntarily given.

Conclusion: Thus, the search for the gun was likely reasonable based on consent, regardless of whether or not it was legitimate based on checkpoint rules for the cops to remove him from his car.

iii) The Plain-View Doctrine: It appears, either because the entire checkpoint process was constitutional, or because D gave his consent to be moved from the car after a constitutionally permissible checkpoint stop, that the stop and seizure was constitutional at the time Dan got out of the car. Thus, the police were constitutionally on solid ground when Dan was out of the car. The plain-view doctrine allows police who are legitimately in a place and see something criminal in plain-view to use that plain-view finding in court. The justification is that a person does not have a reasonable expectation of privacy in something the person lets the public see. Here, the gun will qualify under the plain-view doctrine. The police need not rely on any Terry type frisks of automobiles, or the automobile exception, because they do not apply. The gun was in plain-view, and to the extent that the officer "searched" the car by looking in the window, the plain-view exception applies.

iv) CONCLUSION: The search and seizure was reasonable and the gun should be admissible. The checkpoint rule may validate the entire process, but even if it doesn't then the checkpoint rule was at least legitimate up until the time D was asked to exit the car. Because he consented, there is no violation of the 4th amendment. The gun is admissible based on the plain-view doctrine.

B. Will D prevail on 5th Amendment Miranda Grounds? The 5th Amendment protects the right against self-incrimination. Miranda v. Arizona, a case based on this right, holds that a person's statements made cannot be used against him in court if the Miranda warning is not given. However, Miranda applies only to custodial interrogations, and not when a person is not in custody or voluntarily offers information. Miranda warnings include the right to remain silent, the right to counsel, the knowledge that counsel will be provided to a person, and the knowledge that anything said while in custody may be used against that person in court.

i) No Miranda Warnings were given. Here, the cops gave no warnings. Thus, D's statement is protected if it was made during a custodial interrogation.

a. Custodial. Custodial situations are those in which a reasonable, innocent person does not feel free to terminate the encounter and leave at will. Here, D was out of his car being asked in the company of some police. It seems up to this point to have been a pretty friendly encounter, with the cops not showing much force or intimidation. Still, it's hard to say whether someone would reasonably feel at this point justified and correct in telling the police that this interview has to stop, and that the person is just going to drive away; especially before the sobriety check is performed. Thus, it's a close call. However, as D is out of his car, speaking to police, and about to be subject to a sobriety test, I would conclude that this is a custodial situation as a reasonable person would not feel free to terminate the questioning and leave.

b. Interrogation: An interrogative question is one that is reasonably likely to elicit an incriminating response. This is a pretty close call as well. On one hand, the officers had no indication that the gun was criminally possessed, and thus a mere question about it may not be enough to reasonably expect an incriminating response. On the other hand, if the gun was criminally possessed, then a truthful response would be incriminating. However, because the officer questioned D about the gun without any suspicion at all of it being stolen, I would find this to be a non-interrogative question. I.e., if they knew that there was a stolen gun around, and then they asked, that would be more likely to be an incriminating response. Here, this just seems like the officers inquiring about a gun in the car without any suspicion whatsoever. Thus, Dan's statement should be admissible. It also appears that even if he had denied the ownership of the gun, the bit about him admitting to the crime was completely volunteered. I.e., the cops did not ask him whether he stole the gun. They asked him if he owned it. Thus, D's answer could have been "No." Instead, and completely unprompted, D volunteered that he stole the gun.

ii) CONCLUSION: This was likely a custodial situation. The situation probably not interrogative, but it may have been. Even if it was not an interrogative scenario, D's statement that "I stole the gun" was not in response to any questioning by the police, and is voluntary and admissible. If it is found to be an custodial interrogative situation, the only part of the statement that will be inadmissible will be the answer to the policeman's question: "No."

2. **Which theft crime will D be convicted of?**

A. Theft crimes are specific intent crimes. This means that the thief must specifically intend the proscribed conduct - i.e., the thief must have the mens rea to permanently deprive the true owner of the object possession. Theft crimes include larceny (trespassory taking and carrying away of the personal property of another with intent to permanently deprive); larceny by false pretenses (larceny, plus getting actual title to the property by intentional and legitimate fraud); larceny by trick (larceny, but obtaining mere possession of the property by trick or deception); and embezzlement (the fraudulent conversion of the personal property of another by one legally in possession of that property).

B. No larceny crime lies: This will be an embezzlement, if it's anything. The reason is because the larceny crimes all require an intent to steal the item at the moment of possession. Here, Dan did not form the intent to keep the gun until he had already been in legitimate and lawful possession - as a courier for the church, and holding it for the church. The continuing trespass doctrine will not apply, because that applies to scenarios where a person has borrowed something against the owner's intent, but doesn't plan to steal it until later. That person is never in lawful possession. Because Dan's specific intent mens rea was not formed at the moment of possession of the gun, no larceny crime will lie.

C. Embezzlement: Embezzlement is:
i) Fraudulent: I.e., wrongful. Here, D was supposed to deliver the gun to the church, but has kept the gun. Thus, he is in wrongful possession of the gun at the time the gun was found on him.

ii) Conversion: This means the intent to permanently deprive the owner (Church) of possession. This will be the major issue. Dan tells the cops he wanted to give the gun back; further we have no indication that he ever meant to keep the gun forever - maybe he just wanted to drive around with it for a little bit. Because this is a specific intent crime, the prosecution will have a tough job proving that Dan subjectively and specifically intended to keep the gun forever when he decided to not turn it in. It is important to note that once he kept the gun with intent to steal it, the crime was complete - it doesn't matter if he later developed the intent to return it. The prosecution could point to the fact that he was driving around with it and didn't turn it in when he was supposed to, which may help; so will the statement that "I stole it." This will be the issue at trial, right now it looks only probably proven at best.

iii) Of the personal property of another: The woman gave the gun to the church. As such, the gun was the property of the church.

iv) By someone in legal possession: Dan worked for the church, and it was his job in this instance to deliver the gun to the church. Thus, he has legal possession of the gun when the woman gave it to him. She gave it to him thinking he was going to give it to the church, because he was an employee of the church. The church charged him with the duty of taking donations and delivering them to it. Thus, this possession was legal. It is akin to a bank manager stealing money that he or she is supposed to be counting.

D. CONCLUSION: Embezzlement may lie, but only if the prosecution can prove specific intent to steal the gun, which will be tough.

3. **General conclusion: Gun and statement ("I stole it.") admissible. Embezzlement if there is specific intent, which there likely is.**

ANSWER B TO QUESTION 6

1. <u>Motion to suppress</u>

The fourth amendment prohibits unreasonable searches and seizures by the state. Miranda v. Arizona requires that warnings be given to an individual subject to "custodial interrogation" in order to protect the individual's right to be protected from self-incrimination. This is clearly state action, so the issues here are whether the gun was seized pursuant to an unreasonable search or seizure, or whether the statement was obtained in the context of custodial interrogation.

<u>Exclusionary Rule and Fruit of the poisonous tree doctrine</u>

The exclusionary rule requires that a court exclude evidence seized pursuant to an unlawful search or seizure. The fruit of the poisonous tree doctrine also provides that evidence that is obtained as a result of an lawful search must also be excluded, subject to certain exceptions. The exclusionary rule also requires the suppression of statements obtained in violation of Miranda, although the fruit of the poisonous tree doctrine does not apply to Miranda. Here, if the gun was seized during an unlawful search or seizure, or if the statement was obtained in violation of Miranda, this evidence must be suppressed.

<u>Gun</u>
<u>Expectation of privacy</u>

An individual has standing to challenge a search or seizure when they have a reasonable expectation of privacy in the place or property being searched. When an individual knowingly exposes something to the public, he no longer has standing to challenge a search of it. In this case, Dan placed the gun on the front seat of his car. It is not clear if his windows were tinted, or if someone could see easily into the car and see the gun. However, typically an individual has an expectation of privacy as to the inside and contents of their car, so Dan probably has standing to challenge the search. He certainly has standing to challenge any detention of his person, which would constitute a seizure if a reasonable person would not feel free to leave.

Routine checkpoint

Routine sobriety checkpoints are not considered seizures under the 4th amendment, so long as they are administered in a nondiscretionary manner and do not detain individuals for an unreasonable period of time. In this case, the officers at the checkpoint were stopping all cars, and were asking all drivers to briefly exit before going on their way. As a result, this checkpoint was not a seizure of Dan or his car, and did not implicate the 4th amendment.

Consent

In addition, a search or seizure is not unreasonable if an individual consents to the search. Valid consent must be knowingly and voluntarily given. Whether an individual validly consented is determined objectively, and the court considers whether a reasonable police officer would believe that the individual consented to the search or seizure. In this case, the police officer explained the procedure and asked if Dan would exit the vehicle. As a result, Dan appears to be informed about the procedure and his consent was knowing. His consent was also voluntary because he said okay, and stepped out of the car. A reasonable police officer would consider this to be valid consent.

Plain-View

The plain-view doctrine provides that where a police officer has a right to be in the place that he is, any objects in plain view may be validly searched or seized if there is probable cause to believe that the objects are products or instrumentalities of a crime. In this case, the officer had the right to be in the place that he was, as discussed above, because he had the right to stop Dan pursuant to the nature of the checkpoint and Dan's consent. At this time, the gun was in plain-view. The officer then asked Dan if the gun was his, and he responded that it was stolen. At that time, the police officer had not yet searched or seized the gun because he had not touched it or moved it in any way. However, when Dan confessed that it was stolen, probable cause arose for the officer to seize it, and the seizure was therefore lawful under the plain view doctrine.

Even if the statements were elicited in the context of a Miranda violation (to be discussed below), because the poisonous tree doctrine does not apply to Miranda, and because the gun was in plain view, the seizure of the gun was still lawful.

Dan's motion to suppress the gun is likely to fail.

Statement

A statement is obtained in violation of Miranda where an individual is in custody, and an officer is interrogating the individual without first providing the appropriate Miranda warnings. Here, it is clear that the officer did not provide Miranda warnings, so the question is whether Dan was in custody and whether the police officers question as to whether Dan owned the gun constituted interrogation.

Custody

An individual is in custody for the purposes of Miranda where a reasonable person in his position would not feel free to leave and end the detention. However, the supreme court has specifically held that routine traffic stops did not constitute custody for the purposes of Miranda. In this case, therefore, the routine security checkpoint would not be considered custody for Miranda purposes. It does not matter that Dan thought that he had no choice, because the test is objective, and not subjective. When the police officer asked Dan if he would consent, it is also possible that a reasonable person in Dan's position would have interpreted this question as indicating that he was free to not consent.

Because Dan was not in custody at the time that he made the statement, it was not illicit in violation of Miranda and is admissible.

Interrogation

A police officer is considered to be interrogating an individual where his questions are reasonably likely to illicit incriminating statements. Here, the officer asked Dan if he was the owner of the gun. This question does not seem designed to lead to an incriminating statement, only to determine who was the owner of the gun. In responding to the question, Dan would have been expected to give a simple yes or no. In the event of a non, probably a statement about who it belonged to would be expected. From the perspective of the officer, it probably seemed unlikely that this question would illicit a confession to the theft of the gun.

Because Dan was not being interrogated at the time he made the statement, it was not obtained in violation of Miranda for this reason as well. Dan's motion to suppress the statement is likely to fail.

2. **Likelihood of conviction**
Elements of theft

Larceny, or theft, is the taking or concealing of the property of another with the intent to permanently deprive the owner or rightful possessor of that property of the property. The issue here is whether Dan took property that belonged to the church, and whether he intended to permanently deprive the church of the gun.

Taking

A taking of the property of another occurs where the defendant physically moves the property of another, or conceals it on his person. In this case, although Dan may have had a right to possess the gun at the time that the woman handed it to him, it belonged to the Church as soon as the woman handed it over and told Dan that she wanted the Church to have it. Although Dan may have intended to give the gun to the church, a taking of the gun occurred when he did not give it to the church and instead placed it in his car. When he turned over the book and mislead the church as to the donation, his right of possession did not continue to exist and his action met the first element of larceny.

Intent to permanently deprive

A defendant need not have had the intent to permanently deprive the owner or rightful possessor at the time that the taking of the property occurred. It is enough that the intent to permanently deprive arose after the taking. In this case, it is not clear if

Dan had the intent to permanently deprive. It would appear that he did not intend to ever give the gun to the church when he gave them only the book and placed the gun in his car. This is circumstantial evidence of an intent to permanently deprive and may be sufficient to meet the requirements for this element. On the other hand, he also told the officer that he was planning on giving it back. If he merely later changed his mind about the gun, this would be irrelevant, because if he had the requisite intent even this would be enough. However, this statement could also be circumstantial evidence indicating that he never had the required intent. This is a question for the jury to decide, depending on whether they believe the defendant's statements.

Mistake of law

Dan appears to believe that he "stole the gun." His beliefs about the illegality of his actions are immaterial however. His statement would be relevant only to determine whether he had an intent to permanently deprive. This is because belief that one completed an unlawful act that is actually lawful does not render the act unlawful.

Embezzlement

Embezzlement is a type of theft, and is the taking of a piece of property that the defendant had a right to possess at the time of the taking. Therefore, even if Dan had a right to possess the gun at the time, Dan could still be convicted of embezzlement, as opposed to basic theft. This conviction would turn on whether the jury found that placing the gun in the car was sufficient to indicate that Dan intended to convert the Church's property into his own and permanently deprive the church of it.

Because Dan took a gun that he did not have a right to possess, and because circumstantial evidence indicates he intended to permanently deprive the church of the gun, he is likely to be convicted at trial for theft.